201

CHOCOLATE
TREATS

· ·

201

CHOCOLATE TREATS

Velvety and
Voluptuous Cakes,
Cookies, Pies and More

201 Delicious Recipes
201 Tantalizing Pictures

GREGG R. GILLESPIE

Photographs by Peter Barry

BLACK DOG
& LEVENTHAL
PUBLISHERS
NEW YORK

Published by
Black Dog & Leventhal Publishers, Inc.
151 West 19th Street
New York, NY 10011

Distributed by
Workman Publishing Company
708 Broadway
New York, NY 10003

Printed and bound in Great Britain by
Butler & Tanner, Ltd., Frome & London

Gillespie, Gregg., 1934-
201 chocolate treats : velvety and voluptuous cakes, cookies, pies and more / by Gregg R. Gillespie.
p. cm.

ISBN 1-57912-118-7
1. Cookery (Chocolate) 2. Desserts. I. Title: Two hundred one chocolate treats. II.
TX767.C5 G553 2001
646.6'374--dc21

2001025058

Cover design by Kathy Herlihy-Paoli
Interior design by Design Duo

j i h g f e d c b

TABLE OF CONTENTS

ALMOND FUDGE CAKE

YIELD: *16 servings*
BAKING TIME: *70 minutes*

CAKE
3 ounces unsweetened chocolate, grated or finely chopped
2 cups all-purpose flour
1 (3.4 ounces) package chocolate instant pudding mix
¾ cup semi-sweet chocolate chips
1 teaspoon baking powder
¼ teaspoon cream of tartar
½ teaspoon salt
1½ cups slivered almonds
½ cup butter or margarine, at room temperature
1⅓ cups granulated sugar
2 large eggs
¾ cup sour cream
1 teaspoon almond extract
1 teaspoon amaretto
1 cup Chocolate Frosting V (see page 123)

1 Position a rack in the center of the oven and preheat the oven to 350 degrees. Lightly grease and flour a 10-inch tube pan.

2 To make the cake, melt the chocolate. Remove from the heat.

3 Combine the flour, pudding mix, chocolate chips, baking powder, cream of tartar, and salt.

4 Sprinkle ¾ cup of the almonds in the bottom of the prepared pan.

5 In a large bowl, using an electric mixer on medium speed, beat the butter and sugar until fluffy. Beat in the eggs. Beat in the sour cream, almond extract, and amaretto. Pouring it in a thin stream, beat in the melted chocolate. Beat in the dry ingredients. Fold in the remaining ¾ cup almonds. Pour the mixture into the prepared pan and spread evenly.

6 Bake for 60 to 70 minutes, or until a cake tester inserted into the center comes out clean. Cool in the pan on a wire rack.

7 Make the frosting.

8 Invert the cake onto a serving plate. Spread the frosting on the top and sides of the cake.

Amore – the ITALIANO LOVE CAKE

YIELD: *16 servings*
BAKING TIME: *35 minutes*
CHILL TIME: *20 to 30 minutes*

CAKE
1¼ cups powdered sugar, sifted
1 cup cake flour
15 large egg whites (1½ cups)
1½ teaspoons cream of tartar
1½ teaspoons vanilla or
  chocolate extract
¼ teaspoon almond extract
¼ teaspoon salt
1 cup granulated sugar

FILLING AND TOPPING
½ cup amaretto
1 pint pistachio ice cream, softened
1 pint chocolate ice cream, softened
2 cups heavy cream
1 cup (6 ounces) semi-sweet
  chocolate chips for garnish

1 Position a rack in the center of the oven and preheat the oven to 375 degrees.

2 To make the cake, combine the powdered sugar and cake flour.

3 In a large bowl, using, an electric mixer on high speed, beat the egg whites, cream of tartar, vanilla extract, almond extract, and salt until well mixed and soft peaks form. Beat in the sugar, a little at a time, and beat until stiff but not dry. With a rubber spatula, fold in the dry ingredients until the flour is just incorporated. Pour the mixture into an ungreased 10-inch tube pan, shaking the pan lightly.

4 Bake for 30 to 35 minutes, or until a cake tester inserted into the center comes out clean. Invert the pan onto a bottle or funnel and cool completely.

5 To assemble, using a serrated knife, cut the cake into 3 layers. Sprinkle each of the layers with some of the amaretto. Place one layer on a serving plate. Spread the pistachio ice cream on the bottom layer and top with the second layer. Spread the chocolate ice cream on the second layer and top with the third layer. Freeze the cake for 20 to 30 minutes, or until set.

6 To make the topping, in a chilled bowl, using an electric mixer on medium speed, beat the heavy cream and the remaining amaretto until it forms soft peaks. Spread on the top and sides of the cake. Return to the freezer.

7 In a small saucepan, over low heat, melt the chocolate chips, stirring until smooth. Line a baking sheet with aluminium foil. Pour the melted chocolate onto the prepared pan, spreading it ¼ inch thick. Let chocolate set for 15 minutes. Using an oiled heart-shaped cookie cutter, cut out hearts. Place them on top of the cake. Keep cake in the freezer until ready to serve.

Baked fudge cake

Yield: *12 to 15 servings*
Baking time: *25 minutes*

4 ounces unsweetened chocolate,
   grated or finely chopped
⅓ cup butter or margarine
2 large eggs
1 cup granulated sugar
½ cup all-purpose flour
½ cup chopped walnuts
1 teaspoon chocolate or
   vanilla extract
Pinch of salt
1½ to 2 cups Chocolate Fudge
   Frosting II (see page 123)
   for garnish

1 Position a rack in the center of the oven and preheat the oven to 350 degrees. Lightly grease a 13 by 9-inch pan. Line the bottom of the pan with greased waxed paper.

2 In the top of a double boiler, over simmering water, melt the chocolate and butter, stirring until smooth. Remove from heat.

3 In a large bowl, using an electric mixer on high speed, beat the eggs until thick and light-colored. Beat in the sugar. Beat in the chocolate mixture. Stir in the flour, walnuts, chocolate extract, and salt. Pour the mixture into the prepared pan and spread evenly.

4 Bake for 20 to 25 minutes, or until a cake tester inserted into the center comes out clean. Cool in the pan on a wire rack for 10 minutes. Invert onto a platter to cool completely.

5 Make the frosting. Spread the frosting over the top and sides of the cake.

Black forest cheesecakes

Yield: *24 servings*
Baking time: *25 minutes*
Chill time: *45 minutes*

24 chocolate wafer cookies
1¼ cups granulated sugar
⅓ cup Dutch processed cocoa powder
2 tablespoons all-purpose flour
16 ounces cream cheese, at room
   temperature
3 large eggs
1 cup sour cream or chocolate
   flavored yogurt
½ teaspoon almond extract
½ cup heavy cream
1 can (14 ounces) cherry pie filling

1 Position a rack in the center of the oven and preheat the oven to 325 degrees. Line twenty-four 3-inch muffin-pan cups with aluminium foil baking cups. Place a cookie in the bottom of each cup.

2 Combine the sugar, cocoa powder, and flour.

3 In a large bowl, using an electric mixer on medium-high speed, beat the cream cheese until smooth. Beat in the dry ingredients. Beat in the eggs, one at a time, beating well after each addition. Beat in the sour cream and almond extract. Spoon the mixture into the prepared pans, filling each cup three-quarters full.

4 Bake for 20 to 25 minutes, or until a cake tester inserted into the center comes out clean. Cool in the pan on racks for 10 minutes.

5 In a medium bowl, using an electric mixer on high speed, whip the cream until stiff peaks form. Spread a tablespoon of the whipped cream over the top of each cooled cupcake. Chill 30 to 45 minutes, or until ready to serve. Place a dab of the cherry pie filling in the center of the whipped cream just before serving.

Baking notes: For a variation, use any type of preserved fruit or fruit compote in place of the cherry pie filling.

Banana split cake

YIELD: *12 to 15 servings*
BAKING TIME: *5 minutes*
CHILL TIME: *2 hours*

CRUST
1⅔ cups graham cracker crumbs
¼ cup granulated sugar
⅓ cup vegetable shortening

FILLING
4 medium bananas, sliced
1 cup (6 ounces) semi-sweet
　chocolate chips
1 pint fudge ripple or chocolate
　ice cream, softened

TOPPING
1⅓ cups evaporated milk
1 cup (6 ounces) semi-sweet
　chocolate chips
½ cup butter or margarine
½ teaspoon vanilla or chocolate
　extract
1 cup heavy cream
2 tablespoons chopped pecans
　for garnish
¼ cup fruit cocktail, well drained,
　for garnish

1 Position a rack in the center of the oven and preheat the oven to 375 degrees. Lightly grease a 13 by 9-inch pan.

2 To make the crust, in a medium bowl, combine the crumbs and sugar. Using a pastry blender, cut in the shortening until it forms a crumbly mixture. Press onto the bottom of the prepared pan.

3 Bake for 5 minutes, or until a cake tester inserted into the center comes out clean. Cool on a wire rack.

4 To make the filling, cover the baked crust with the sliced bananas in a single layer. Sprinkle with the chocolate chips and spread the ice cream over the top. Chill in the freezer for 1 hour.

5 To make the topping, in a saucepan, over a medium heat, combine the milk, chocolate chips, and butter. Bring to a boil, reduce heat to low, and simmer for 5 minutes, or until mixture thickens slightly. Remove from the heat and stir in the vanilla extract. Cool completely. Spread over the chilled ice cream layer and freeze for 1 hour.

6 In a medium bowl, using an electric mixer on medium-high speed, beat the cream until soft peaks form. Spread the whipped cream over the top of the cake and garnish with the nuts and fruit. Serve immediately.

BAKING NOTES: **For a special occasion, make the dessert in a fancy oven-proof bowl or in a springform pan. Chocolate whipped cream (see page 125) can be used in place of the plain whipped cream.**

BROWNIE PEANUT BUTTER CHEESECAKE

YIELD: *16 servings*
BAKING TIME: *47 minutes*
CHILL TIME: *Overnight*

CRUST
3½ ounces semi-sweet chocolate, grated or finely chopped
¼ cup butter or margarine
½ cup all-purpose flour
⅛ teaspoon baking powder
2 large eggs
1 cup packed light-brown sugar
1½ teaspoons chocolate extract

FILLING
12 ounces cream cheese, at room temperature
1 cup packed light-brown sugar
3 large eggs
½ cup sour cream or yogurt
1⅓ cups creamy peanut butter

TOPPING
¾ cup sour cream or yogurt
2 teaspoons granulated sugar
½ cup creamy peanut butter
Small apricot roses for garnish (see page 121)

1 Position a rack in the center of the oven and preheat the oven to 350 degrees. Lightly grease and flour a 9 or 10-inch springform pan.

2 To make the crust , in the top of a double boiler over simmering water, melt 3 ounces of the chocolate and the butter, stirring until smooth. Remove from the heat.

3 Combine the flour and baking powder.

4 In a medium bowl, using an electric mixer on medium speed, beat the eggs until thick and light-colored. Beat in the brown sugar until well blended. Beat in the melted chocolate, chocolate extract, and remaining ½ ounce grated chocolate. Gradually stir in the dry ingredients, mixing just until blended. Spread 1 cup evenly onto the bottom of the prepared pan. Chill the remaining crust mixture.

5 Bake for 15 to 17 minutes, or until a cake tester inserted into the center comes out clean. Cool in the pan in the refrigerator for 15 to 30 minutes.

6 To make the filling, in a large bowl, using an electric mixer on medium speed, beat the cream cheese and brown sugar until smooth. Beat in the eggs and sour cream. Beat in the peanut butter.

7 To prepare the pan, use a spatula to spread the remaining chilled crust mixture evenly around the insides of the pan. To make this easier, set the pan on its side and roll it, spreading at the same time. Pour in the filling mixture.

8 Bake 25 to 30 minutes, or until a cake tester inserted into the center comes out clean. Spread the topping on the cheesecake about 3 minutes before removing from the oven.

9 To make the topping, in a small bowl, using an electric mixer on medium speed, mix the sour cream, sugar, and peanut butter until smooth. Cool on a wire rack for 1 hour. Place in a plastic or paper bag and chill overnight.

10. Remove the side of the pan and garnish with the small apricot roses. Cut the cake into narrow wedges and serve.

BROWNSTONE
CHOCOLATE CAKE

YIELD: *10 to 12 servings*
BAKING TIME: *60 minutes*

2 ounces unsweetened chocolate,
  grated or finely chopped
1 cup boiling water
1 teaspoon amaretto
2 cups all-purpose flour
1 teaspoon baking soda
¼ teaspoon salt
3 large eggs
½ cup sour cream or yogurt
¼ cup butter or margarine,
  at room temperature
1¼ cups packed light-brown sugar
1⅔ cups Custard Filling
  (see page 126)
¾ cup Strawberry Glaze
  (see page 128)
Sliced fresh strawberries or
  chocolate-dipped strawberries
  for garnish

1 Position a rack in the center of the oven and preheat the oven to 350 degrees. Lightly grease and flour a 9 by 5-inch loaf pan.

2 In a small bowl, combine the chocolate and boiling water, stirring until chocolate is melted and smooth. Add the amaretto.

3 Combine the flour, baking soda, and salt.

4 In a medium bowl, using an electric mixer on medium speed, beat the eggs, sour cream, and chocolate mixture until smooth.

5 In a large bowl, using an electric mixer on medium-high speed, beat the butter and brown sugar until fluffy. In three additions, mix in the dry ingredients, alternating with the chocolate mixture, beginning and ending with the dry ingredients. Pour the mixture into the prepared pan and spread evenly.

6 Bake for 55 to 60 minutes, or until a cake tester inserted into the center comes out clean. Cool completely in the pan on a wire rack.

7 Make the custard filling and strawberry glaze.

8 To assemble, using a serrated knife, slice the cake in half horizontally. Place the bottom layer on a serving platter and spread with the custard filling. Top with the second layer and pour strawberry glaze over the top. Garnish with the sliced strawberries or strawberries dipped in chocolate.

Chocolate angel food cake I

YIELD: *16 servings*
BAKING TIME: *65 minutes*

CAKE
1¼ cups granulated sugar
1 cup cake flour
¼ cup Dutch processed cocoa powder
15 large egg whites (1½ cups)
½ teaspoon salt
1½ teaspoons cream of tartar
1 teaspoon coffee liqueur
¼ teaspoon chocolate
   or vanilla extract

FROSTING
3 tablespoons powdered sugar
2 tablespoons Dutch processed cocoa
   powder
1 cup heavy cream
½ teaspoon crème de cacao
Chocolate Curls or Chocolate Leaves
   (see page 128) for garnish

1 Position a rack in the center of the oven and preheat the oven to 325 degrees.

2 To make the cake, in a medium bowl, combine the sugar, cake flour, and cocoa powder. Sift two times.

3 In a large bowl, using an electric mixer on high speed, beat the egg whites and salt until foamy. Sprinkle the cream of tartar over the top and continue beating until stiff but not dry. Fold in the dry ingredients, blending until just mixed. Fold in the coffee liqueur and chocolate extract. Pour the mixture into an ungreased 10-inch tube pan, and spread evenly.

4 Bake for 60 to 65 minutes, or until a cake tester inserted into the center comes out clean. Invert the pan onto a wire rack or stand it on its tube and cool completely.

5 To make the frosting, combine the powdered sugar and cocoa powder.

6 In a medium bowl, using an electric mixer on medium-high speed, beat the cream to soft peaks. Fold in the dry ingredients. Fold in the crème de cacao. Chill well before using.

7 Invert the cake on a serving plate. Spread the frosting over the entire cake and garnish with chocolate curls or chocolate leaves.

BAKING NOTES: **The cake can also be split into layers and filled. Using a serrated knife, cut the cake horizontally into three layers. Use the chocolate whipped cream as a filling and sprinkle cocoa sugar over the top (see page 125).**

Chocolate
BUTTER CAKE

Yield: *12 servings*
Baking time: *35 minutes*

CAKE
3 ounces unsweetened chocolate,
    grated or finely chopped
2 cups all-purpose flour
1 teaspoon baking powder
¼ teaspoon cream of tartar
½ teaspoon salt
½ cup butter or margarine,
    at room temperature
1⅓ cups granulated sugar
2 large eggs
¾ cup sour cream
1 teaspoon vanilla or
    chocolate extract

FILLING AND FROSTING
2 cups powdered sugar
1 cup vegetable shortening
1 teaspoon chocolate syrup
1½ cups Chocolate Rum Icing
    (see page 124)

1 Position a rack in the center of
the oven and preheat the oven to
350 degrees. Lightly grease and
flour two 9-inch round cake pans.

2 To make the cake, melt the
chocolate. Remove from the heat.

3 Combine the flour, baking powder,
cream of tartar, and salt.

4 In a large bowl, using an electric
mixer on high speed, beat the butter and sugar until light and fluffy.
Beat in the eggs. Beat in the sour
cream and vanilla extract. Beat in
the melted chocolate. Divide the
mixture and pour into the two
prepared pans and spread evenly.

5 Bake for 30 to 35 minutes, or
until a cake tester inserted into the
center comes out clean. Cool in the
pans on wire racks for 10 minutes.
Invert onto the racks to cool completely.

6 To make the filling, in a medium
bowl, using an electric mixer on
medium speed, beat the powdered
sugar, shortening, and chocolate
syrup until smooth and spreadable.

7 Make the icing.

8 To assemble, place one cake
layer on a serving plate and spread
evenly with the filling. Place the
second layer on top and frost the
top and sides of the cake with the
icing.

Chocolate
CHOCOLATE TORTE

Yield: *10 to 12 servings*
Baking time: *1 hour*

FLOURLESS CHOCOLATE CAKE
8 ounces semi-sweet chocolate,
**   grated or finely chopped**
1½ tablespoons butter or margarine
5 large eggs
¼ cup granulated sugar
⅓ cup dark corn syrup
CHOCOLATE GLAZE
¾ cup heavy cream
8 ounces semi-sweet chocolate,
**   grated or finely chopped**
1½ tablespoons butter or margarine,
**   at room temperature**
1½ tablespoons dark corn syrup
Paper-thin slices of orange for
**   garnish**

1 Position a rack in the center of the oven and preheat the oven to 350 degrees. Grease and flour a 9-inch round cake pan and line the bottom with waxed or parchment paper. Grease and flour the paper.

2 In the top of a double boiler over simmering water, melt the chocolate and butter, stirring until smooth. Remove from the heat.

3 In a large bowl, using an electric mixer on high speed, beat the eggs and sugar until thick and light-colored. Beat in the corn syrup. Pouring it in a thin stream, beat in the chocolate mixture on low speed. Pour the mixture into the prepared pan and spread evenly.

4 Bake for 1 hour, or until a cake tester inserted into the center comes out clean. Cool in the pan on a wire rack. Invert onto a serving plate.

5 To make the glaze, in a saucepan over low heat, warm the cream for 1 minute. Reduce the heat even lower and add the chocolate. Stir constantly until the chocolate is melted and the mixture is smooth. Remove from the heat. Let stand just until cool. Using a wire whisk, beat in the butter and corn syrup. Spread the glaze over the top and sides of the torte. Garnish with orange slices.

Chocolate
CREAM TORTE

Yield: *10 to 12 servings*
Baking time: *25 minutes*
Chill time: *3 hours*

CHOCOLATE TORTE
4 ounces semi-sweet chocolate,
   grated or finely chopped
1½ tablespoons strong brewed coffee
¾ teaspoon chocolate extract
4 large eggs, separated
Pinch of salt
½ cup granulated sugar

CHOCOLATE ALMOND FILLING
2 ounces semi-sweet chocolate,
   grated or finely chopped
2 large egg whites
¼ cup granulated sugar
1 tablespoon amaretto
¼ cup ground almonds

WHIPPED CREAM TOPPING
½ cup heavy cream
1½ teaspoons powdered sugar
¼ cup ground almonds
1 ounces semi-sweet chocolate,
   grated or finely chopped
Melted semi-sweet chocolate
   for garnish
6 to 8 Chocolate Leaves
   (see page 128) for garnish

1 Position a rack in the center of the oven and preheat the oven to 350 degrees. Lightly grease two 8-inch square pans. Line the bottoms of the pans with waxed or parchment paper. Grease the paper.

2 In the top of a double boiler over simmering water, combine the chocolate and coffee, stirring constantly until the chocolate is melted and the mixture is smooth. Remove from the heat and stir in the chocolate extract.

3 In a large bowl, using an electric mixer on high speed, beat the egg whites and salt until foamy. Gradually add the sugar and beat until stiff but not dry.

4 In another large bowl, using an electric mixer on medium speed, beat the egg yolks until thick and light-colored. Stir in the chocolate mixture. Fold in the egg whites,

one-third at a time, blending after each addition until white streaks no longer appear. Divide the mixture and pour into the two prepared pans and spread evenly.

5 Bake for 20 to 25 minutes, or until a cake tester inserted into the center comes out clean. Cool in the pans on wire racks for 5 minutes. Invert onto the racks to cool completely.

6 To make the filling, melt the chocolate. Remove from the heat.

7 In a large bowl, using an electric mixer on high speed, beat the egg whites until foamy. Gradually add the sugar and beat until stiff but not dry. Fold in the amaretto, almonds, and melted chocolate. Chill until ready to use.

8 To make the topping, in a medium bowl, using an electric mixer on high speed, whip the cream and powdered sugar until stiff peaks form. Fold in the almonds and grated chocolate.

9 To assemble, using a serrated knife, cut the two layers in half horizontally to make four layers. Place one of the layers on a serving plate and spread with one-third of the filling. Top with a second layer. Repeat the layers of cake and filling, ending with the fourth cake layer. Spread the top cake layer with the whipped cream topping. Garnish with a drizzle of melted chocolate and chocolate leaves. Chill for 2 to 3 hours before serving.

Baking notes: An alternative garnish is fresh fruit, such as sliced strawberries, whole raspberries, peeled and sliced kiwifruit, or sliced lemon or orange.

Chocolate
EUPHORIA CAKE

Yield: *12 servings*
Baking time: *30 minutes*

CAKE

2½ ounces unsweetened chocolate,
    grated or finely chopped
2 cups all-purpose flour
1 teaspoon baking soda
¼ cup butter or margarine,
    at room temperature
2 cups granulated sugar
2 large eggs
1 cup buttermilk
1 teaspoon chocolate or vanilla
    extract
2 tablespoons cider vinegar

FROSTING

5 ounces semi-sweet chocolate,
    grated or finely chopped
½ cup butter or margarine,
    at room temperature
2 cups powdered sugar
⅓ cup evaporated milk
1 teaspoon vanilla or chocolate extract
½ teaspoon salt

1 Position a rack in the center of the oven and preheat the oven to 350 degrees. Lightly grease and flour an 8-inch round cake pan.

2 Melt the chocolate. Remove from the heat.

3 Combine the flour and baking soda.

4 In a large bowl, using an electric mixer on high speed, beat the butter and sugar until light and fluffy. Beat in the eggs. Beat in the buttermilk, chocolate extract, and vinegar. Pouring it in a thin stream, beat in the melted chocolate. Gradually blend in the dry ingredients. Pour the mixture into the prepared pan and spread evenly.

5 Bake for 25 to 30 minutes, or until a cake tester inserted into the center comes out clean. Cool in the pan on a wire rack 10 minutes. Invert onto the rack to cool completely.

6 To make the frosting, melt the chocolate. Remove from the heat.

7 In a large bowl, using an electric mixer on high speed, beat the butter and powdered sugar until light and fluffy. Beat in the evaporated milk, vanilla extract, and salt. In a steady stream, beat in the melted chocolate.

8 Invert the cake onto a serving plate. Spread the frosting evenly on the top and sides of the cake.

Chocolate
FUDGE CAKE I

YIELD: *12 servings*
BAKING TIME: *35 minutes*
FREEZING TIME: *1 hour*

CAKE
10 large eggs, separated
1 tablespoon distilled white vinegar
1 tablespoon water
1¼ cups granulated sugar
7 ounces unsweetened chocolate,
    grated or finely chopped
3 ounces semi-sweet chocolate,
    grated or finely chopped
¾ cup butter or margarine, a
    t room temperature
4½ teaspoons coffee liqueur
    (see Baking notes)
4½ teaspoons baking powder
FILLING
4½ tablespoons instant coffee
    powder
6 tablespoons hot water
3 ounces unsweetened chocolate,
    grated or finely chopped
1½ cups butter or margarine
3 cups powdered sugar, sifted
4 large egg yolks
GLAZE
9 tablespoons water
6 tablespoons butter or margarine
3 tablespoons canola oil
3 tablespoons unsweetened
    chocolate, grated or finely chopped
9 tablespoons granulated sugar
1 cup Dutch processed cocoa powder
2 tablespoons Kahlúa
    (see Baking notes)
White Chocolate Leaves
    (see page 128) for garnish
Fresh chrysanthemums for garnish

1 Position a rack in the center of
the oven and preheat the oven to
350 degrees. Lightly grease and
flour three 9-inch round cake pans.
Line the bottoms with waxed or
parchment paper and butter the
paper.

2 To make the cake, in a large
bowl, using an electric mixer on
high speed, beat the egg whites
until foamy. Gradually add the
vinegar and water, beating on high
speed until the whites hold stiff
peaks.

3 In the top of a double boiler over
simmering water, combine the
sugar and chocolates, stirring constantly until the chocolate is melted
and the mixture is smooth. Remove
from the heat. Using a metal spoon,
beat in the butter and liqueur until
smooth.

4 In another large bowl, using an
electric mixer on medium speed,
beat the egg yolks until thick and
light-colored. Beat in the baking
powder. Pouring it in a thin
stream, beat in the chocolate mixture. Fold in the egg whites, one-
fourth at a time, blending until no
white streaks remain. Divide the
mixture and pour into the three
prepared pans and spread evenly.

5 Bake for 30 to 35 minutes, or
until a cake tester inserted into the
center comes out clean. Cool in the
pans on wire racks for 10 minutes.
Invert onto the racks to cool completely. The cakes will sink in the
center as they cool.

6 To make the filling, in the top of
a double boiler over simmering
water, combine the coffee powder,
hot water, and chocolate, stirring
constantly until the chocolate is
melted and the mixture is smooth.
Remove from the heat.

7 In a medium bowl, using an
electric mixer on medium speed,
beat the butter and powdered
sugar until thick and smooth. Beat
in the egg yolks. Add the chocolate
mixture and beat until a thick and
spreadable consistency is achieved.

Fast 'n easy CHOCOLATE SHEET CAKE

YIELD: *12 servings*
BAKING TIME: *35 minutes*

8 To make the glaze, in a medium saucepan, bring the water, butter, and oil to a boil. Remove from the heat and cool slightly. Stir in the chocolate, sugar, cocoa powder, and Kahlúa. Beat with an electric mixer on low speed until the mixture is very thick.

9 To assemble, remove the waxed paper, and invert one cake layer onto a serving plate. Spread the layer with half of the filling and top with a second cake layer. Spread with the remaining filling and invert the last layer on top. Smooth out any filling that has oozed between the layers. Freeze for 1 hour, or until solid.

10 Pour the glaze over the frozen cake and let it drip down the sides. Smooth out the glaze on the sides and let the cake stand at room temperature to defrost. Garnish with white chocolate leaves and fresh white chrysanthemums before serving.

BAKING NOTES: The liqueur and Kahlúa should be used at room temperature so they will blend more easily with the chocolate. Plastic or silk flowers can be used in place of the fresh chrysanthemums.

1 package (3.4 ounces) cook-and-serve chocolate pudding mix
1 box (18.5 ounces) chocolate cake mix
2 cups semi-sweet chocolate chips
1 cup chopped walnuts for garnish

1 Position a rack in the center of the oven and preheat the oven to 350 degrees. Lightly grease an 11½ by 17½-inch sheet pan. Line the pan with waxed or parchment paper and grease the paper.

2 Make the pudding mix according to the package directions and pour into a large mixing bowl. Gradually blend in the cake mix. Pour the mixture into the prepared pan and spread evenly. Sprinkle the chocolate chips over the top.

3 Bake for 30 to 35 minutes, or until a cake tester inserted into the center comes out clean. Spread the melted chocolate chips evenly over the top of the cake and sprinkle the walnuts on top. Cool in the pan on a wire rack. Invert cake onto the rack to cool completely. Cut into squares.

Good guys' CHOCOLATE CAKE

YIELD: *12 to 15 servings*
BAKING TIME: *35 minutes*
CHILL TIME: *30 minutes*

2½ cups all-purpose flour
1 teaspoon baking soda
Pinch of salt
4 ounces unsweetened chocolate, grated or finely chopped
½ cup water
2 cups granulated sugar
1 cup vegetable shortening
4 large eggs
1 cup buttermilk
1 teaspoon vanilla or chocolate extract
1¼ cups warm Chocolate Syrup II (see page 125) for topping
2 cups whipped topping for garnish
3 candy bars (8 ounces each), crushed, for garnish

1 Position a rack in the center of the oven and preheat the oven to 350 degrees. Lightly grease and flour a 13 by 9-inch pan.

2 Combine the flour, baking soda, and salt.

3 In the top of a double boiler over simmering water, combine the chocolate and water, stirring until smooth.

4 In a large bowl, using an electric mixer on medium speed, beat the shortening and sugar until fluffy. Beat in the eggs, one at a time. Beat in the buttermilk and vanilla extract. Pouring it in thin stream, beat in the chocolate mixture. Gradually blend in the dry ingredients. Pour the mixture into the prepared pan and spread evenly.

5 Bake for 30 to 35 minutes, or until a cake tester inserted into the center comes out clean. Cool in the pan on a wire rack for 10 minutes. Using a large fork, poke holes 1½ inches apart all over the top of the cake. Pour the chocolate syrup over the warm cake and cool completely. Chill for 30 minutes before serving.

6 To serve, spread the whipped topping over the top of the cake and sprinkle with the crushed candy bars.

GRASSHOPPER CHEESECAKE

YIELD: *12 servings*
BAKING TIME: *40 minutes*
CHILL TIME: *30 minutes*

CRUST
1½ cups chocolate wafer cookie crumbs
1 tablespoon granulated sugar
2 tablespoons butter or margarine, melted
FILLING
16 ounces cream cheese, at room temperature
1 cup granulated sugar
3 large eggs
¼ cup green crème de menthe
2 tablespoons crème de cacao
TOPPING
3 ounces semi-sweet chocolate, grated or finely chopped
½ cup sour cream or yogurt

1 Position a rack in the center of the oven and preheat the oven to 350 degrees. Lightly grease an 8-inch springform pan.

2 To make the crust, in a small bowl, combine the cookie crumbs, sugar, and the melted butter. Press firmly onto the bottom and up to an inch on the sides of the prepared pan. Chill.

3 To make the filling, in a large bowl, using an electric mixer on medium speed, beat the cream cheese and sugar until smooth. Beat in the eggs. Continue beating until the mixture is very smooth. Stir in the crème de menthe and crème de cacao. Pour into the chilled crust.

4 Bake for 35 to 40 minutes, or until a cake tester inserted into the center comes out clean. Cool in the pan on a wire rack.

5 To make the topping, melt the chocolate. Remove from the heat and cool slightly.
Stir in the sour cream. Spread over the top of the cooled cheesecake. Chill 30 minutes, or until serving.

6 Remove the side of the pan and place the cheesecake on a serving plate.

Italian almond torte

Yield: *10 to 12 servings*
Baking time: *25 minutes*

⅔ cup almonds, finely ground
3 ounces unsweetened chocolate, grated or finely chopped
½ cup amaretto or almond wafer cookie crumbs
1 teaspoon baking powder
Pinch of salt
6 large eggs, separated
1 cup granulated sugar
1 teaspoon almond extract
1 teaspoon crème de cacao or chocolate extract
Pinch of cream of tartar
2 cups Chocolate Whipped Cream (see page 125)
Chocolate Curls (see page 122) for garnish

1 Position a rack in the center of the oven and preheat the oven to 350 degrees. Lightly grease and flour two 9-inch round cake pans.

2 In a medium bowl, combine the nuts, grated chocolate, cookie crumbs, baking powder, and salt.

3 In a large bowl, using an electric mixer on medium speed, beat the egg yolks until thick and light-colored. Gradually beat in ¾ cup of the sugar. Beat in the almond extract and crème de cacao.

4 In another large bowl, using an electric mixer on high speed, beat the egg whites and cream of tartar until foamy. Gradually beat in the remaining ¼ cup sugar and beat until stiff but not dry. Fold in the egg yolks, one-fourth at a time. Fold in the dry ingredients. Divide the mixture and pour into the two prepared pans and spread evenly.

5 Bake for 20 to 25 minutes, or until a cake tester inserted into the center comes out clean. Cool in the pans on wire racks to cool completely.

6 To assemble, using a serrated knife, cut each layer in half horizontally to make four layers. Place one layer on a serving plate and spread with ½ cup of the chocolate whipped cream. Top with a second cake layer. Repeat the layers until all four cake layers are used, ending with a layer of whipped cream. Garnish with chocolate curls.

ICE WATER CHOCOLATE CAKE

YIELD: *12 to 15 servings*
BAKING TIME: *40 minutes*

2 ounces unsweetened chocolate,
  grated or finely chopped
2 cups all-purpose flour
1 teaspoon baking soda
1 teaspoon salt
2 large eggs, separated
1 teaspoon cream of tartar
½ cup butter-flavored vegetable
  shortening
1½ cups granulated sugar
1 cup ice water
1 teaspoon chocolate or almond
  extract
1 cup Chocolate Almond Sauce
  (see page 121)
Seasonal fresh fruit for garnish

1 Position a rack in the center of the oven and preheat the oven to 350 degrees. Lightly grease a 13 by 9-inch pan.

2 Melt the chocolate. Remove from the heat.

3 Combine the flour, baking soda, and salt.

4 In a small bowl, using an electric mixer on high speed, beat the egg whites until foamy. Add the cream of tartar and beat until stiff peaks form.

5 In a large bowl, using an electric mixer on medium speed, beat the shortening and sugar until fluffy. Beat in the egg yolks. Beat in the melted chocolate. Beat in the ice water and chocolate extract. Gradually beat in the dry ingredients. Fold in the egg whites. Pour the mixture into the prepared pan and spread evenly.

6 Bake for 35 to 40 minutes, or until a cake tester inserted into the center comes out clean. Cool in the pan on a wire rack.

7 Make the glaze.

8 Invert the cake onto a serving plate. Spread the glaze on the top and sides of the cake. Garnish with fruit.

MARSHMALLOW FUDGE CAKE

YIELD: *12 to 15 servings*
BAKING TIME: *35 minutes*

CAKE
1½ cups butter or margarine
3 ounces semi-sweet chocolate,
  grated or finely chopped
1½ cups all-purpose flour
1 teaspoon baking powder
4 large eggs
1 cup granulated sugar
2 teaspoons chocolate or vanilla extract
2 cups miniature marshmallows

TOPPING
½ cup butter or margarine
2 ounces unsweetened chocolate
  grated or finely chopped
½ cup evaporated milk or heavy cream
1 teaspoon coffee liqueur
2 cups powdered sugar

1 Position a rack in the center of the oven and preheat the oven to 350 degrees. Lightly grease a 13 by 9-inch pan.

2 In the top of a double boiler over simmering water, combine the butter and chocolate, stirring occasionally until chocolate is melted and the mixture is smooth. Remove from the heat.

3 Combine the flour and baking powder.

4 In a large bowl, using an electric mixer on medium speed, beat the eggs and sugar until thick and light-colored. Gradually blend in the dry ingredients. Stir in the chocolate extract. Fold in the melted chocolate. Pour the mixture into the prepared pan and spread evenly.

5 Bake for 30 to 35 minutes, or until a cake tester inserted into the center comes out clean. Spread the marshmallows over the top and cool in the pan on a wire rack.

6 To make the topping, in the top of the double boiler over simmering water, combine the butter and chocolate, stirring until chocolate and butter is melted and the mixture is smooth. Stir in the milk and coffee liqueur. Simmer for 2 minutes, remove from the heat, and stir in the powdered sugar.

7 Invert cake onto a serving plate. our the hot topping over the marshmallows on the cake. Cool completely. Cut into squares.

MISSISSIPPI MUD CAKE I

YIELD: *16 servings*
BAKING TIME: *90 minutes*

2 cups all-purpose flour
1 teaspoon baking soda
Pinch of salt
5 ounces unsweetened chocolate,
  grated or finely chopped
1¾ cups strong brewed coffee
¼ cup bourbon
1 cups butter or margarine,
  at room temperature
2 cups powdered sugar
2 large eggs, beaten
1 teaspoon vanilla extract
2 cups Chocolate Coconut Frosting
  (see page 121) for garnish

1 Position a rack in the center of
the oven and preheat the oven to
275 degrees. Lightly grease and
flour a 10-inch tube pan.

2 Combine the flour, baking soda,
and salt.

3 In the top of a double boiler over
simmering water, combine the
chocolate with the coffee, stirring
until smooth. Remove from the
heat and stir in the bourbon.

4 In a large bowl, using an electric
mixer on medium speed, beat the
butter and powdered sugar until
light and fluffy. Slowly beat in the
chocolate mixture. Beat in the eggs
and vanilla extract. Gradually
blend in the dry ingredients. Pour
the mixture into the prepared pan
and spread evenly.

5 Bake for 90 minutes, or until a
cake tester inserted into the center
comes out clean. Cool in the pan
on a wire rack.

6 Make the frosting.

7 Invert the cake onto a serving
plate and spread the frosting over
the top and sides evenly.

OLD ENGLISH CHOCOLATE CAKE

YIELD: *12 servings*
BAKING TIME: *75 minutes*

1 ounce unsweetened chocolate,
  grated or finely chopped
2 tablespoons cornstarch or
  arrowroot
1½ teaspoons water
½ teaspoon all-purpose flour
½ teaspoon baking powder
6 large eggs, separated
1½ cups granulated sugar
3 cups chopped walnuts
2 cups Chocolate Glaze IV
  (see page 123) for garnish
3 tablespoons chopped pecans
  for garnish

1 Position a rack in the center of
the oven and preheat the oven to
375 degrees. Lightly grease a 9-inch
round pan. Line the bottom with
waxed paper and grease the paper.

2 Melt the chocolate. Remove from
the heat.

3 In a cup, dissolve the cornstarch
in the water.

4 Combine the flour and baking
powder.

5 In a large bowl, using an electric
mixer on high speed, beat the egg
whites until stiff but not dry.

6 In a large bowl, using an electric
mixer on medium speed, beat the
egg yolks until thick and light-colored. Beat in the sugar. Beat in the
walnuts, melted chocolate, and
cornstarch mixture. Gradually stir
in the dry ingredients. Fold in the
egg whites. Pour into the prepared
pan and spread evenly.

7 Bake for 60 to 75 minutes, or
until a cake tester inserted into the
center comes out clean. The cake
will split on top. Cool in the pan
on a wire rack for 5 minutes. Invert
onto the rack to cool completely.

8 Make the chocolate glaze.

9 Remove waxed paper and
invert the cake onto a serving dish.
Spread the chocolate glaze over
the top and sprinkle with pecans.

One-egg
CHOCOLATE CAKE

Yield: *12 servings*
Baking time: *40 minutes*

2 cups cake flour
1¼ cups granulated sugar
1 teaspoon baking soda
½ teaspoon salt
½ cup butter-flavored vegetable
  shortening
3 ounces semi-sweet chocolate,
  grated or finely chopped
1 teaspoon chocolate or vanilla
  extract
1 large egg
1 cup buttermilk
1½ cups Fudge Frosting II
  (see page 123)

1 Position a rack in the center of
the oven and preheat the oven to
350 degrees. Lightly grease and
flour two 8-inch round cake pans.

2 Combine the flour, sugar, baking
soda, and salt.

3 In the top of a double boiler
over simmering water, combine the
shortening and chocolate, stirring
until the chocolate is melted and
the mixture is smooth. Remove
from the heat, and using an electric
mixer on medium speed, beat in
the chocolate extract and egg. In
three additions, beat in the dry
ingredients, alternating with the
buttermilk, beginning and ending
with the dry ingredients. Divide
the mixture and pour into the prepared pans and spread evenly.

4 Bake for 35 to 40 minutes, or
until a cake tester inserted into the
center comes out clean. Cool in the
pans on wire racks for 5 minutes.
Invert the cakes onto the racks to
cool completely.

5 Make the Fudge Frosting.

6 To assemble, place the first layer
on a serving platter. Spread the top
and sides of the layer with frosting.
Place the second layer on the top
of the frosting. Spread the frosting
evenly over the top and sides of
the cake.

Passover
nut torte

Yield: *10 to 12 servings*
Baking time: *30 minutes*

¾ cup matzo meal
¾ cup walnuts, very finely ground
¼ cup Dutch processed cocoa powder
4 large eggs, separated
½ teaspoon salt
8 tablespoons granulated sugar
¼ cup honey
¼ cup fresh orange juice
¼ teaspoon ground cinnamon
1 tablespoon Cocoa Sugar
  (see page 125) for garnish
Raspberry Sauce
  (see page 128) for serving

1 Position a rack in the center of
the oven and preheat the oven to
350 degrees. Lightly grease a 9-inch
square pan. Line the bottom with
waxed or parchment paper.

2 Combine the matzo meal,
walnuts, and cocoa powder.

3 In a medium bowl, using an electric mixer on high speed, beat the
egg whites and salt until foamy.
Add 2 tablespoons of the sugar and
beat until stiff but not dry.

4 In a large bowl, using an electric
mixer on medium speed, beat the
egg yolks until thick and light-colored. Gradually add the remaining
6 tablespoons sugar and beat on
high speed for 2 to 3 minutes. Beat
in the honey, orange juice, and cinnamon. Gently fold in the egg
whites, a little at a time, alternating
with the dry ingredients. Pour the
mixture into the prepared pan and
spread evenly.

5 Bake for 25 to 30 minutes, or
until a cake tester inserted into the
center comes out clean. Cool in the
pan on a wire rack for 10 to 12
minutes. Invert onto the rack to
cool completely. Remove the waxed
paper and place on a serving plate.
Sift the cocoa sugar over the top.
Cut into squares and serve with
the sauce on the side.

PISTACHIO PUDDING CHOCOLATE CAKE

YIELD: *12 to 14 servings*
BAKING TIME: *45 minutes*

½ cup chopped pistachios
1 box (18.5 ounces) yellow cake mix
1 package (3.4 ounces) Jell-O Brand pistachio instant pudding mix
1 cup canola oil
½ cup orange juice
3 large eggs
½ cup club soda
¾ cup chocolate syrup
Powdered sugar for garnish

1 Position a rack in the center of the oven and preheat the oven to 350 degrees. Lightly grease and flour a 10-inch Bundt pan. Sprinkle the pistachio nuts evenly over the bottom of the prepared pan.

2 In a large bowl, using an electric mixer on medium speed, beat the cake mix, pudding mix, oil, orange juice, eggs, and club soda until blended. Pour half of the mixture into the prepared pan, being careful not to disturb the pistachio nuts.

3 Add the chocolate syrup to the remaining batter and stir until well blended. Pour over the top of the mixture in the pan. Using a knife, swirl the batters two or three times. Do not overmix or touch the bottom or sides of the pan.

4 Bake for 40 to 45 minutes, or until a cake tester inserted into a light section of the cake comes out clean. Cool in the pan on a wire rack for 15 minutes. Invert onto the rack to cool completely. Place on a serving plate. Sprinkle with powdered sugar.

RED DEVIL'S FOOD CAKE

YIELD: *12 servings*
BAKING TIME: *30 minutes*

2 cups cake flour
1 teaspoon baking soda
¼ teaspoon salt
2 ounces semi-sweet chocolate, grated or finely chopped
½ cup butter or margarine
1½ cups granulated sugar
2 large eggs
1 teaspoon chocolate or vanilla extract
½ cup buttermilk
½ cup boiling water
1 tablespoon Cocoa Sugar (see page 125) for garnish

1 Position a rack in the center of the oven and preheat the oven to 350 degrees. Lightly grease two 8-inch round cake pans. Line the bottoms with waxed or parchment paper. Butter the paper and flour the pans.

2 Combine and sift the flour, baking soda, and salt.

3 In the top of a double boiler over simmering water, combine the chocolate and butter, stirring until chocolate is melted and the mixture is smooth. Remove from the heat and stir in the sugar.

4 In a large bowl, using an electric mixer on medium speed, beat the eggs until thick and light-colored. Pouring it in a thin stream, beat in the chocolate mixture. Beat in the chocolate extract. Combine the buttermilk and boiling water. In three additions, blend in the dry ingredients, alternating with the buttermilk mixture, beginning and ending with the dry ingredients. Beat until well blended. The batter will be thin. Divide the mixture and pour into the prepared pans and spread evenly.

5 Bake for 25 to 30 minutes, or until a cake tester inserted into the center comes out clean. Cool for 5 minutes in the pans on wire racks. Invert onto the racks to cool completely.

6 Sprinkle with cocoa sugar.

Swiss almond torte

Yield: *12 to 14 servings*
Baking time: *12 minutes*

ALMOND CAKE
6 large eggs, separated
¾ cup granulated sugar
1 cup almonds, finely ground
½ cup all-purpose flour
2 teaspoons amaretto

CHOCOLATE FROSTING
4 ounces unsweetened chocolate, grated or finely chopped
2 large eggs
1½ cups granulated sugar
1½ cups butter or margarine, at room temperature
1 teaspoon almond extract

ASSEMBLY
½ cup sliced almonds
¼ cup apricot preserves
1 teaspoon crème de cacao

1 Position two racks in the oven: one in the top third and the other in the bottom third. Preheat the oven to 375 degrees. Line two 15½ by 10½-inch jelly-roll pans with waxed or parchment paper.

2 To make the cake, in a large bowl, using an electric mixer on high speed, beat the egg whites until foamy. Add ¼ cup of the sugar and beat until stiff peaks form.

3 In another large bowl, using an electric mixer on medium speed, beat the egg yolks with the remaining ½ cup sugar until thick and light-colored. Add the ground almonds, flour, and amaretto. Fold the beaten egg whites into the egg yolk mixture. Divide the mixture and pour into the two prepared pans and spread evenly.

4 Bake for 12 minutes, or until a cake tester inserted into the center comes out clean, switching the pans' positions in the oven after 6 minutes. Immediately invert the cakes and remove the waxed paper. Using a serrated knife, cut each cake into four 4 by 11-inch strips. Cool the strips on wire racks.

5 To make the frosting, melt the chocolate. Remove from the heat.

6 In a medium saucepan, using an electric mixer on medium speed, beat in the eggs and sugar until blended. Cook over low heat, stirring constantly for 3 minutes. Remove from the heat. Add the melted chocolate, butter, and almond extract and beat until the butter is melted and the mixture is smooth. Cover and chill until a spreadable consistency.

7 To assemble, spread half of the chocolate frosting on seven of the strips of cake. Stack the strips on a serving plate and top with the unfrosted strip of cake. Frost the top and sides with the remaining chocolate frosting. Press the sliced almonds onto the sides of the torte. Mix the apricot preserves and crème de cacao and spread on the top. Chill until ready to serve.

BAKING NOTES: If you only have one 15½ by 10½-inch pan, bake half of the batter at a time, relining the pan with waxed paper and baking the second cake as soon as the first one is out of the pan.

TUNNEL OF FUDGE CAKE

YIELD: *16 servings*
BAKING TIME: *60 minutes*

2½ cups chocolate frosting mix
2 cups all-purpose flour
2 cups walnuts, finely chopped
1½ cups butter or margarine, at room temperature
1½ cups granulated sugar
6 large eggs
Powdered sugar for garnish

1 Position a rack in the center of the oven and preheat the oven to 350 degrees. Grease and flour a 10-inch Bundt pan.

2 Combine the frosting mix, flour, and walnuts.

3 In a large bowl, using an electric mixer on medium speed, beat the butter and sugar until light and fluffy. Beat in the eggs, one at a time, beating until smooth and light-colored. Gradually blend in the dry ingredients. Pour the mixture into the prepared pan and spread evenly.

4 Bake for 55 to 60 minutes, or until the cake pulls from the sides of the pan. The cake will appear soft in the center. Cool in the pan on a wire rack for at least 1 hour.

5 Invert the cake onto a serving plate. Sprinkle the top of the cake with powdered sugar.

TRIPLE CHOCOLATE CAKE I

YIELD: *16 servings*
BAKING TIME: *45 minutes*
CHILL TIME: *90 minutes*

1⅓ cups cake flour
1 cup semi-sweet chocolate chips
½ cup Dutch processed cocoa powder
1 package (3.4 ounces) Jell-O Brand chocolate instant pudding mix
1 teaspoon baking powder
½ teaspoon baking soda
¼ teaspoon salt
6 tablespoons vegetable shortening
1 cup granulated sugar
3 large eggs
1½ teaspoons crème de cacao
½ cup Coffee Mocha Icing I (see page 126)
¾ pint chocolate ice cream

1 Position a rack in the center of the oven and preheat the oven to 350 degrees. Lightly grease and flour a 10-inch Bundt or tube pan.

2 Combine the flour, chocolate chips, cocoa powder, pudding mix, baking powder, baking soda, and salt.

3 In a large bowl, using an electric mixer on medium speed, beat the shortening and sugar until fluffy. Beat in the eggs. Beat in the crème de cacao. Gradually blend in the dry ingredients. Pour the mixture into the prepared pan and spread evenly.

4 Bake for 40 to 45 minutes, or until a cake tester inserted into the center comes out clean. Cool in the pan on a wire rack for 10 minutes. Invert onto the rack to cool completely. Chill the cake for 1 hour.

5 Make the mocha frosting.

6 To assemble, place the cake on a serving plate. Spread the frosting on the top and sides of the cake. Fill the hole in the center of the cake with ice cream. Freeze for 30 minutes or until ready to serve.

WHITE CHOCOLATE CAKE I

YIELD: *12 servings*
BAKING TIME: *35 minutes*

2½ cups all-purpose flour
1 cup pecans or walnuts, coarsely
    chopped
1 cup flaked coconut
1 teaspoon baking soda
5 ounces white chocolate,
    grated or finely chopped
½ cup boiling water
4 large eggs, separated
1 cup butter or margarine,
    at room temperature
2 cups granulated sugar
2 teaspoons vanilla extract
1 cup buttermilk
2 cups Coffee Mocha Icing
    (see page 126)
Thinly sliced limes for garnish
Fresh mint sprigs for garnish

1 Position a rack in the center of the oven and preheat the oven to 350 degrees. Lightly grease and flour three 9-inch round cake pans.

2 Combine the flour, pecans, coconut, and baking soda.

3 In a small bowl, combine the white chocolate and boiling water, stirring until smooth.

4 In a small bowl, using an electric mixer on high speed, beat the egg whites until stiff but not dry.

5 In a large bowl, using an electric mixer on medium speed, beat the butter and sugar until light and fluffy. Beat in the egg yolks. Beat in the vanilla extract and buttermilk.

Gradually blend in the dry ingredients. Fold in the beaten egg whites. Divide the mixture and pour into the three prepared pans and spread evenly.

6 Bake for 30 to 35 minutes, or until a cake tester inserted into the center comes out clean. Cool in the pans on wire racks for 5 minutes. Invert onto the racks to cool completely.

7 Make the mocha frosting.

8 To assemble, place one cake layer on a serving plate and spread with some of the frosting. Place the second cake layer on top and spread with frosting. Top with the third cake layer and spread frosting on the top and sides of the cake. Garnish with mint sprigs and lime slices.

ALMOND BRITTLE

YIELD: *1¹/₂ to 2 pounds*

CHOCOLATE-COATED GINGER

YIELD: *1¹/₂ pounds*

2 cups granulated sugar
⅔ cup water
⅓ cup light corn syrup
¼ cup butter or margarine
½ cup unsweetened chocolate, grated or finely chopped
1 teaspoon chocolate extract
½ teaspoon baking soda
1½ cups almonds, coarsely chopped

1 Grease 15½ by 10½-inch jelly-roll pan.

2 In a saucepan, over medium heat, combine the sugar, water, corn syrup, and butter. Insert a candy thermometer and cook, without stirring, until 300 degrees. Remove from the heat. Quickly stir in the chocolate, chocolate extract, baking soda, and almonds. Pour the mixture onto the prepared pan and spread it out to the sides of the pan. Cool in the pan until hard. Break into pieces.

BAKING NOTES: The secret of this recipe is to spread the brittle very thinly.

8 ounces semi-sweet chocolate, grated or finely chopped
1 pound crystallized ginger, cut into bite-size cubes

1 Melt the chocolate. Remove from the heat.

2 Insert a toothpick into each cube of ginger. Dip the ginger in the chocolate and set on a waxed paper-lined baking sheet to harden. Use as hors d'oeuvres.

BAKING NOTES: If many pieces of ginger are to be coated with chocolate, use a flat piece of Styrofoam as a holder for the toothpicks while the chocolate hardens. Skewer each piece of ginger with a toothpick, dip it into the melted chocolate, and insert the other side of the toothpick into the foam.

Chocolate-covered Bananas

Yield: *12 servings*

6 medium bananas
1 cup semi-sweet chocolate chips
2 tablespoons butter or margarine
12 wooden Popsicle™ sticks
½ cup pecans, finely chopped

1 Peel the bananas and cut in half. Insert a wooden stick into the small end and place on a waxed paper-lined baking sheet. Freeze for 2 to 3 hours, or until hard.

2 In the top of a double boiler over simmering water, melt the chocolate chips and butter, stirring until smooth.

3 Dip the frozen bananas into the chocolate and roll in the pecans. Freeze until the chocolate is hard. Serve or wrap in plastic wrap and freeze until serving.

Chocolate covered Cherries II

Yield: *10 to 15 cherries*
Freeze time: *1 hour*

1 jar (8 ounces) maraschino cherries with stems, drained
1/2 cup fresh orange juice, strained
1 teaspoon maraschino liqueur
3 ounces semi-sweet chocolate, grated or finely chopped

1 Place the cherries in a small bowl. Add the orange juice and liqueur. Let stand for 30 minutes. Cover and freeze for 1 hour.

2 Melt the chocolate. Remove from the heat.

3 Drain the frozen cherries and wipe dry with paper towels. Dip the frozen cherries in the chocolate. Place each cherry on a waxed paper-lined baking sheet. Let stand at room temperature until firm. Place in the refrigerator until hard.

BAKING NOTES: Any kind of liqueur can be used in place of the maraschino liqueur. Coating chocolate may also be used in place of the semi-sweet chocolate listed above.

Chocolate apple slices

YIELD: *approximately 12 pieces*

3 firm medium apples
1 cup granulated sugar
1 cup honey
1 teaspoon ground cinnamon
½ cup water
8 ounces semi-sweet chocolate,
  grated or finely chopped

1 Core and peel the apples. Slice horizontally into ½-inch slices. Place in a bowl of cold water.

2 In a medium saucepan, over medium heat, combine the sugar, honey, cinnamon, and water. Bring to a boil. Simmer for 5 minutes, or until reduced by half.

3 Drain the apples and pat them dry between two paper towels. Drop them into the boiling syrup and cook for 3 to 4, or until they look translucent. Place on a wire rack for 5 minutes, or until cool and dry.

4 To coat the apple slices, melt the chocolate. Remove from the heat. Using a bamboo skewer or a fondue fork, dip each apple slice into the chocolate and place on a waxed paper-lined baking sheet. Cool until firm.

Chocolate creams

YIELD: *2½ to 3 pounds*
CHILL TIME: *1 hour*

2 pounds milk chocolate,
  grated or finely chopped
1 cup heavy cream
1 recipe Dipping Chocolate
  (see page 126)

1 Lightly grease a 13 by 9-inch pan.

2 To make the cream centers, melt the chocolate. Transfer the melted chocolate to a large bowl.

3 In a small saucepan, over low heat, using a candy thermometer, heat the cream to 130 degrees. Add the hot cream to the chocolate. Using an electric mixer on medium speed, whip for 3 to 5 minutes, or until thickened. Cover with a damp cloth and freeze for 5 to 8 minutes, or until thickened. Whip on medium speed for 3 to 5 minutes, or until thicker. Pour into the prepared pan and chill 1 hour, or until just set.

4 Using a teaspoon or melon baller, scoop up the chocolate mixture and roll into ¾-inch balls. Place on a waxed paper-lined baking sheet and refrigerate until ready to use.

5 Make the dipping chocolate.

6 To dip, using a bamboo skewer or a fondue fork, dip the centers into the dipping chocolate, coating them completely. Place the coated centers on a waxed paper-lined baking sheet. Keep in the refrigerator.

Chocolate-dipped Almonds

YIELD: *36 almonds*

2 ounces semi-sweet chocolate,
  grated or finely chopped
1 tablespoon plus 1 teaspoon
  butter or margarine
3 dozen raw whole almonds

1 Line a baking sheet with waxed paper.

2 In the top of a double boiler over simmering water, melt the chocolate and butter, stirring until smooth. Remove from the heat.

3 Dip only half of each almond in the chocolate and place on the prepared baking sheet. Chill until set. Dip the other half of each almond in the chocolate if desired and chill until set.

Chocolate Fondant

YIELD: *2 to 2½ pounds*

3 ounces unsweetened chocolate,
  grated or finely chopped
¾ cup water
2 cups granulated sugar
2 tablespoons light corn syrup
⅛ teaspoon salt
½ teaspoon chocolate
  or vanilla extract

1 In a saucepan over low heat, melt the chocolate with the water, stirring until smooth. Add the sugar, corn syrup, and salt, stirring until the sugar is dissolved. Insert a candy thermometer and bring the mixture to a boil. Cook, stirring, until 236 degrees. Immediately pour onto a cold marble slab and cool to 110 degrees, without touching. Alternatively, pour into a 13 by 9-inch pan and place the pan in water that is at room temperature.

2 Using a metal spatula, work the fondant in an over-and-under folding motion until cool. When cool enough to handle, knead until smooth. Knead in the chocolate extract and let stand, uncovered, until cool. Wrap in waxed paper or plastic wrap until ready to use.

BAKING NOTES: The fondant can be rolled into balls, or molded and dipped in chocolate as desired.

Chocolate Orange Truffles

YIELD: *12 to 16 truffles*
CHILL TIME: *1 hour*

12 ounces semi-sweet chocolate,
   grated or finely chopped
4 tablespoons butter or margarine,
   at room temperature
½ teaspoon cup fresh orange juice,
   strained
1 tablespoon grated orange zest
1 cup walnuts, chopped for coating

1 Melt the chocolate. Remove from the heat and place in a medium bowl. Using an electric mixer on medium speed, beat in the butter until fluffy. Beat in the orange juice and zest. Cover and chill until firm.

2 Using a tablespoon or melon baller, scoop up the truffle mixture and roll it into 1-inch balls. Roll each truffle in the chopped nuts until well coated. Place in self-sealing plastic bags and freeze until serving.

Chocolate Fudge with Cherries

YIELD: *1½ pounds*

2 cups granulated sugar
1 cup milk
½ teaspoon teaspoon salt
2 ounces unsweetened chocolate,
   grated or finely chopped
2 tablespoons butter or margarine
1 teaspoon crème de cacao
½ teaspoon cup walnuts, chopped
¼ cup candied cherries,
   finely chopped

1 Lightly grease a 13 by 9-inch pan.

2 In a saucepan over low heat, combine the sugar, milk, and salt, stirring until blended. Stir in the chocolate. Bring to a boil, stirring occasionally. Insert a candy thermometer and cook until 234 degrees. Remove from the heat and stir in the butter. Cool to 130 degrees.

3 Stir in the crème de cacao. Return to the heat and cook over medium heat until the mixture starts to thicken. Remove from the heat and cool. Fold in the walnuts and cherries. Immediately pour into the prepared pan and spread evenly. Cool until set. Cut into squares.

Chocolate fudge with walnuts

Yield: 1¼ to 1½ pounds

2 cups granulated sugar
1 cup water
1 cup sweetened condensed milk
3 ounces unsweetened chocolate, grated or finely chopped
1 cup chopped walnuts

1 Lightly grease a 9-inch square pan.

2 In a heavy large saucepan, over medium heat, combine the sugar and water. Bring to a boil and simmer for 1 minute. Stir in the condensed milk. Insert a candy thermometer and cook until 235 degrees, stirring occasionally. Remove from the heat and cool for 10 to 15 minutes. Add the chocolate and walnuts. Using a wooden spoon, beat until thick. Pour into the prepared pan and spread evenly. Cool until set. Cut into squares.

BAKING NOTES: For thinner pieces of fudge, use a 13 by 9-inch pan.

Chocolate hazelnut clusters

Yield: 2 pounds

9 ounces semi-sweet chocolate, grated or finely chopped
1½ cups hazelnuts
1 teaspoon instant espresso powder
1 teaspoon canola oil

1 Line a baking sheet with waxed paper.

2 Melt the chocolate. Remove from the heat. Add the hazelnuts, espresso powder, and oil and stir until the nuts are well coated.

3 Drop the mixture by teaspoonfuls onto the prepared baking sheet. Let cool at room temperature until set. Store in an airtight container.

Chocolate Marzipan Logs

YIELD: 1¾ to 2 pounds
CHILL TIME: 6 hours

Chocolate Marzipan Truffles

YIELD: 1 to 1½ pounds
CHILL TIME: 90 minutes

12 ounces sweetened chocolate, grated or finely chopped
½ cup heavy cream
¼ cup powdered sugar
7 ounces marzipan

1 Melt 6 ounces of the chocolate. Remove from the heat.

2 In a small saucepan, over medium heat, bring the cream to a rolling boil. Whisk the cream into the melted chocolate. Pour the mixture into a large bowl, cover, and let stand at room temperature until thickened (about 3 hours).

3 On a flat surface dusted with powdered sugar, roll the marzipan out into a 12 by 6-inch rectangle. With a sharp knife, trim the rough edges, and cut in half to make two 12 by 3-inch rectangles. Place each rectangle on a waxed paper-lined baking sheet.

4 Fill a pastry bag fitted with a large plain tip with the cooled chocolate mixture. Pipe a straight line of the mixture lengthwise down each of the marzipan rectangles, leaving a ¼-inch border on the top and bottom. Moisten one long edge of each rectangle and roll the marzipan up and over the chocolate, sealing to enclose the cream. Cover the logs with waxed paper or plastic wrap and chill for at least 3 hours.

5 Melt the remaining 6 ounces of chocolate. Remove from the heat. Using a dry pastry brush, paint the chocolate over the length of the logs. Let stand at room temperature until the chocolate is firm. Cut into ½ to ¾-inch slices. Chill until serving.

12 ounces semi-sweet chocolate, grated or finely chopped
1 pound marzipan
½ cup hazelnuts, finely ground
1 tablespoon amaretto
¼ cup Dutch processed cocoa powder for coating

1 Melt the chocolate. Remove from the heat.

2 In a large bowl, crumble the marzipan. Beat in the melted chocolate to form a smooth paste. Blend in the hazelnuts and amaretto. Cover and refrigerate for 30 minutes, or until thick but not firm.

3 Using a teaspoon or melon baller, scoop up the mixture and roll it into 1-inch balls. Roll each truffle in the cocoa powder until well coated. Chill for 1 hour or until firm before serving.

CHOCOLATE NUT CRUNCH

YIELD: *1½ pounds*

CHOCOLATE PEPPERMINT CANDY

YIELD: *¾ to 1 pound*
CHILL TIME: *1 hour*

1¼ cups granulated sugar
1 cup whole almonds
¾ cup butter or margarine
¼ cup water
1½ teaspoons salt
½ teaspoon baking soda
½ cup chopped walnuts
⅓ cup semi-sweet chocolate chips
½ cup ground almonds

1 Grease a 15½ by 10½-inch jelly-roll pan.

2 In a saucepan, over medium heat, combine the sugar, whole almonds, butter, water, and salt. Bring to a boil. Insert a candy thermometer and simmer, stirring frequently, until 290 degrees.

3 Remove from the heat. Stir in the baking soda and walnuts. Immediately pour into the prepared pan. Sprinkle the chocolate chips over the top. Let stand for 3 minutes. Spread the melted chocolate chips over the top. Sprinkle with the ground almonds. Cool in the pan until set. Break into pieces.

4 ounces semi-sweet chocolate, grated or finely chopped
1½ cups crushed peppermint candies (½ pound)

1 Line a baking sheet with waxed paper.

2 Melt the chocolate. Remove from the heat and stir in the candy.

3 Drop the mixture by teaspoonfuls onto the prepared baking sheet. Chill until firm.

BAKING NOTES: Almost any hard candy that can be crushed can be substituted for the peppermint candy. Do not use a food processor to crush the candy, as this will make a powder out of the candy. Place the candy between two sheets of waxed paper and pound it with a food mallet or the bottom of a heavy pan.

CHOCOLATE TRUFFLES

Yield: 30 to 36 truffles
Chill time: 9 hours

6 ounces milk chocolate, grated or finely chopped
6 ounces semi-sweet chocolate, grated or finely chopped
¾ cup heavy cream
¼ cup butter or margarine
1½ tablespoons crème de cacao
1 recipe Dipping Chocolate (see page 126)
Cocoa powder or chopped nuts for coating

1 In a small bowl, combine the chocolates. Chill until cold.

2 In a small saucepan, over medium heat, warm the cream until bubbles start to form around the sides of the pan. Remove from the heat.

3 In another small saucepan, over low heat, melt the butter and cook until hot to the touch. Remove from the heat.

4 Place the hot butter and cream in the container of a blender and blend on high speed for a few seconds, until smooth. Add the chilled chocolates. Blend on high speed until smooth and incorporated. Pour into a medium bowl and stir in the crème de cacao. Cover and chill for 8 hours.

5 Using a tablespoon or melon baller, scoop up the mixture and roll it into 1-inch balls. Place on a waxed paper-lined baking sheet and freeze until firm.

6 Make the dipping chocolate. Dip each truffle into the chocolate, coating completely. Roll in cocoa powder or chopped nuts. Place on the baking sheet and chill about an hour or until set.

CHOCOLATE VANILLA WAFER COOKIE CANDY

Yield: 1½ to 1¾ pounds
Chill time: 1 hour

4 ounces semi-sweet chocolate, grated or finely chopped
1 can (14 ounces) sweetened condensed milk
2 cups vanilla wafer cookie crumbs
1 teaspoon chocolate or vanilla extract
1 cup pecans, finely chopped
Powdered sugar for coating

1 Lightly grease a 13 by 9-inch pan.

2 In the top of a double boiler over simmering water, melt the chocolate, stirring constantly. Stir in the condensed milk and cook until thickened. Remove from the heat. Stir in the cookie crumbs, chocolate extract, and nuts.

3 Pour the mixture into the prepared pan and spread evenly. Chill for 1 hour, or until set. Cut into squares. Roll each square in powdered sugar. Wrap individually in waxed paper or plastic wrap and chill until serving.

Baking notes: For a variation, chocolate wafer cookie crumbs can be used.

COCOA FUDGE WITH PEANUT BUTTER

Yield: *1½ pounds*

COCONUT CHOCOLATE BALLS

Yield: *1½ pounds*
Chill time: *1 hour*

4 cups granulated sugar
2¼ cups evaporated milk or
  heavy cream
¾ cup water
¾ cup Dutch processed cocoa powder
1 jar (16 ounces) creamy style
  peanut butter
1 teaspoon chocolate or vanilla
  extract

1 Lightly grease a 13 by 9-inch pan.

2 In a large saucepan, over medium heat, combine the sugar, evaporated milk, water, and cocoa powder. Bring the mixture to boil. Insert a candy thermometer and cook, stirring occasionally, until 244 to 248 degrees. Remove from the heat and cool to 110 degrees.

3 Stir in the peanut butter and the chocolate extract. Using a wooden spoon, beat until slightly more cooled. Pour into the prepared pan and cool completely until set. Cut into squares.

8 ounces milk chocolate,
  grated or finely chopped
4 ounces semi-sweet chocolate,
  grated or finely chopped
8 ounces flaked coconut
2 cups rice crispy cereal

1 Line a baking sheet with waxed paper.

2 In the top of a double boiler over simmering water, melt the chocolates, stirring until smooth. Remove from the heat. Stir in the coconut and cereal.

3 Butter or oil your hands and roll tablespoons of the mixture into small balls. Place the balls on the prepared baking sheet. Chill 1 hour or until firm.

Coquetier le chocolat

YIELD: *8 servings*
CHILL TIME: *30 minutes*

8 ounces semi-sweet chocolate,
   grated or finely chopped
8 miniature foil candy cups
¾ cup crème de cacao

1 Place the foil candy cups on a
tray and freeze for 10 minutes.

2 Melt the chocolate. Remove from
the heat.
Pour some of the chocolate into
each chilled cup. Tilt and move the
cups around to coat the sides with
chocolate. Freeze for 30 minutes or
until hardened.

3 Carefully peel the cup from the
hardened chocolate. Fill the chocolate cups with crème de cacao.
Serve with after dinner coffee.

Coffee-chip fudge

YIELD: *3 pounds*

3 cups granulated sugar
1 cup milk
½ cup half-and-half
2 tablespoons light corn syrup
2 tablespoons instant espresso
   powder
Pinch of salt
3 tablespoons butter or margarine
1 teaspoon almond extract
1 cup semi-sweet chocolate chips
½ cup chopped almonds

1 Lightly grease an 8 or 9-inch
square pan.

2 In a large saucepan, over low
heat, combine the sugar, milk,
half-and-half, corn syrup, espresso
powder, and salt. Stirring until
smooth, bring to a boil. Insert a
candy thermometer and cook,
without stirring, until 236 degrees.
Remove from the heat. Add the
butter and almond extract without
stirring and cool to 110 degrees.

3 Using a wooden spoon, beat
until the mixture loses its gloss and
a small amount dropped from a
spoon holds its shape. Stir in the
chocolate chips and nuts. Pour into
the prepared pan and cool until
set. (Do not scrape the sides of the
saucepan.) Cut into squares.

Easy chocolate truffles

YIELD: *5 dozen truffles*
CHILL TIME: *3 hours*

12 ounces semi-sweet chocolate,
  grated or finely chopped
4 ounces cream cheese,
  at room temperature
3 cups powdered sugar
1½ teaspoons chocolate extract
Ground almonds for coating

1 Line two baking sheets with
waxed paper.

2 Melt the chocolate. Remove from
the heat.

3 In a large bowl, using an electric
mixer on medium speed, beat the
cream cheese until smooth. Beat in
the powdered sugar, ½ cup at a
time. Beat in the melted chocolate
and chocolate extract. Cover and
chill for 1 hour or until firm.

4 Pinch off small pieces of the
mixture and roll it into 1-inch balls.
Roll each truffle in the almonds
until well coated. Place on the
prepared baking sheets. Chill for 1
to 2 hours or until serving.

BAKING NOTES: Chopped pecans,
cocoa powder, or toasted coconut
can also be used to coat the truffles.

French chocolate

YIELD: *50 to 60 candies*
CHILL TIME: *2 hours*

1⅓ cups semi-sweet chocolate chips
1 cup walnuts, ground
¾ cup sweetened condensed milk
1 teaspoon crème de cacao
Flaked coconut for coating

1 Line a baking sheet with waxed
paper.

2 Melt the chocolate chips.
Remove from the heat. Stir in the
walnuts, condensed milk, and
crème de cacao. Cool for 5 minutes.

3 Pinch off pieces of the mixture
and roll into 1-inch balls. Roll each
ball in the coconut until well coated. Place the balls on the prepared
baking sheet. Chill for 2 hours before
serving.

BAKING NOTES: Chopped walnuts or
powdered sugar can also be used to
coat the chocolates.

Gregg's chocolate

Yield: *1 pound*

Holiday fudge

Yield: *3¹/₂ pounds*
Chill time: *1 hour*

8 ounces semi-sweet chocolate,
  grated or finely chopped
8 ounces almond bark,
  grated or finely chopped
½ teaspoon water

1 In the top of a double boiler over simmering water, melt the chocolate and almond bark, stirring constantly until smooth. Stir in the water. The mixture will seize. Continue stirring until the mixture forms a gob.

2 Place the mixture between two sheets of waxed paper and roll out to a thickness of ⅜-inch. Cut into squares while still pliable. Allow to stand at room temperature until firm.

Baking notes: A combination of semi-sweet chocolate chips and white chocolate chips or chocolate chips and peanut butter chips can also be used. You also melt the chips separately, and layer one on top of the other before rolling out under the waxed paper. If you use the two layer method, add 1 or 2 drops of peppermint extract to the white chocolate before the water.

2 cups granulated sugar
1 cup heavy cream
¼ cup light corn syrup
2 ounces semi-sweet chocolate,
  grated or finely chopped
2 teaspoons chocolate or vanilla
  extract
1 teaspoon almond extract
1 cup candied cherry halves
1 cup chopped almonds

1 Lightly grease a 9-inch square pan.

2 In a saucepan over low heat, combine the sugar, cream, corn syrup, and chocolate. Bring to a boil, stirring occasionally. Insert a candy thermometer and cook, without stirring, until 238 degrees. Remove from the heat and cool to 110 degrees.

3 Add the chocolate and almond extracts. Using a wooden spoon, beat until thick. Fold in the cherries and almonds. Immediately pour the mixture into the prepared pan and spread evenly. Chill 1 hour or until firm. Cut into squares.

Marshmallow
CHOCOLATE NUT BALLS

Yield: *24 balls*
Chill time: *1 hour*

Mexican
CHOCOLATE TRUFFLES

Yield: *24 truffles*
Chill time: *2 hours*

2 ounces unsweetened chocolate,
  grated or finely chopped
1⅓ cups sweetened condensed milk
24 large marshmallows
1 cup chopped almonds for coating

1 Line a baking sheet with waxed paper

2 In the top of a double boiler over simmering water, melt the chocolate, stirring until smooth. Add the condensed milk and cook for 3 to 5 minutes, or until the mixture thickens.

3 Using a bamboo skewer or a fondue fork, dip the marshmallows in the chocolate mixture, coating completely. Roll in the almonds and place on the prepared baking sheet. Cool for 1 hour or until set.

COATING
¼ cup unsweetened cocoa powder
1½ teaspoons ground cinnamon
TRUFFLES
4 ounces semi-sweet chocolate,
  grated or finely chopped
⅓ cup powdered sugar
⅓ cup almond paste
1 tablespoon strong brewed coffee
1 teaspoon butter or margarine,
  melted

1 To make the coating, on a small plate, combine the cocoa powder and cinnamon.

2 To make the truffles, mix the chocolate, powdered sugar, almond paste, coffee, and butter until it forms a smooth paste. Using a tablespoon or melon baller, scoop up the mixture and roll it into 1-inch balls. Roll each truffle in the coating mixture until well coated. Place on a waxed paper-lined baking sheet and chill for 2 hours before serving.

Baking notes: For a decorative garnish, drizzle melted white or dark chocolate over the truffles. The truffles can also be made in larger sizes.

Mint chocolate fudge

Yield: *1¹/₂ to 2 pounds*
Chill time: *2 hours*

10 ounces semi-sweet chocolate,
grated or finely chopped
1 can (14 ounces) sweetened
condensed milk
2 teaspoons crème de cacao
1 cup white chocolate chips
1 tablespoon peppermint or
spearmint schnapps
3 drops green food coloring

1 Line a 9-inch square pan with
waxed paper.

2 In a large saucepan, over low
heat, melt the semi-sweet chocolate
with 1 cup of the condensed milk,
stirring until smooth. Remove from
the heat and add the crème de
cacao. Pour half of the mixture into
the prepared pan and spread evenly.
Chill for 10 minutes. Keep the
remaining chocolate mixture at
room temperature.

3 In a medium saucepan, over
low heat, melt the white chocolate
chips with the remaining condensed
milk, stirring until smooth.
Remove from the heat and stir in
the schnapps and food coloring.
Spread this mixture over the top
of the chilled chocolate and chill
for 10 minutes or until firm.

4 Spread the remaining chocolate
mixture on top of the white chocolate mixture and chill for 2 hours
or until firm. Invert onto a sheet
of waxed paper and peel off the
waxed paper from the bottom.
Cut into bite-size pieces.

**Baking notes: Crème de menthe can
be used in place of the schnapps.**

Mocha truffles ii

Yield: *1¹/₂ to 2 dozen truffles*
Chill time: *1 hour*

1¹/₄ cups powdered sugar
3 ounces unsweetened chocolate,
grated or finely chopped
½ cup butter or margarine, melted
2 tablespoons coffee liqueur
4 large egg yolks
½ cup Brazil nuts,
finely ground for coating

1 In a medium bowl, combine the
powdered sugar, grated chocolate,
butter, and liqueur. Beat in the egg
yolks, one at a time. Chill for 1
hour, or until the mixture is firm
enough to form into balls.

2 Using a tablespoon or melon
baller, scoop up the mixture and
roll into 1-inch balls. Roll each
truffle in the nuts until well coated.
Place in an airtight container and
chill until serving.

**Baking notes: Due to the raw eggs
used in this recipe, keep refrigerated
at all times, and for no longer than 1
week.**

Nougat squares

Yield: *1½ pounds*
Chill time: *1 hour*

3 tablespoons butter or margarine
1 jar (7 ounces) marshmallow creme
4 cups puffed corn cereal
½ cup flaked coconut
¼ cup ground almonds
½ teaspoon salt
1 cup semi-sweet chocolate chips

1 Lightly grease a 9-inch square pan.

2 In the top of a double boiler over simmering water, melt the butter with the marshmallow creme, stirring until smooth. Remove from the heat. Add the cereal, coconut, almonds, and salt. Press evenly onto the bottom of the prepared pan.

3 In the top of a double boiler over simmering water, melt the chocolate chips, stirring until smooth. Spread evenly over the top of the mixture in the pan. Chill for 1 hour or until set. Cut into bars.

Opera fudge

Yield: *2½ pounds*
Chill time: *1 hour*

3 ounces unsweetened chocolate,
   grated or finely chopped
1 tablespoon light corn syrup
2 cups granulated sugar
¾ cup heavy cream
½ cup evaporated milk
¾ cup pecans, chopped
1 teaspoon chocolate
   or vanilla extract
6 ounces semi-sweet chocolate,
   grated or finely chopped

1 Lightly grease a 9-inch square pan.

2 In a saucepan over low heat, melt the unsweetened chocolate and corn syrup, stirring until smooth. Stir in the sugar, cream, and evaporated milk. Insert a candy thermometer and cook, stirring occasionally, until 238 degrees. Remove from the heat and stir in the pecans and chocolate extract. Pour the mixture into the prepared pan and spread evenly. Cool slightly.

3 Melt the semi-sweet chocolate . As soon as the fudge starts to harden, spread the melted chocolate over the top. Chill for 1 hour or until firm. Cut into bite-size pieces.

Parisian truffles

Yield: *1½ to 2 dozen*
Chill time: *2 hours*

2 ounces semi-sweet chocolate,
   grated or finely chopped
½ cup granulated sugar
1 cup hazelnuts, finely ground
⅓ cup water
2 tablespoons butter or margarine,
   melted
1 teaspoon ground cinnamon
1 recipe Dipping Chocolate
   (see page 126)

1 Line a baking sheet with waxed
or parchment paper.

2 In the top of a double boiler over
simmering water, melt the chocolate, stirring until smooth. Add the
sugar and stir until dissolved.
Remove from the heat. Stir in the
hazelnuts, water, butter, and cinnamon, blending in a slow motion
until smooth. Let cool 30 minutes,
or until almost solid. Using a tablespoon or melon baller, scoop up
the mixture and roll it into 1-inch
balls.

3 Make the dipping chocolate.

4 Using a bamboo skewer or a fondue fork, dip the truffles into the
dipping chocolate, coating completely. Place on a waxed paper-
lined baking sheet. Let cool until
set. Chill for 2 hours before serving.

Peanut butter chocolate fudge

Yield: *2½ pounds*
Chill time: *2 hours*

2 cups peanut butter chips
1 can (14 ounces) sweetened
   condensed milk
¼ cup butter or margarine
½ cup peanuts, chopped
1 cup semi-sweet chocolate chips

1 Line an 8-inch square pan with
waxed or parchment paper.

2 In a medium saucepan, over low
heat, melt the peanut butter chips,
1 cup of the condensed milk, and 2
tablespoons of the butter, stirring
constantly until smooth. Remove
from the heat and immediately stir
in the peanuts. Pour the mixture
evenly in the bottom of the prepared pan.

3 In the top of a double boiler over
simmering water, melt the chocolate chips, stirring constantly until
smooth. Add the remaining condensed milk and butter and stir
until blended. Spread evenly over
the peanut butter layer in the pan.
Chill for 2 hours or until firm.
Invert onto a sheet of waxed paper
and peel off the waxed paper from
the bottom. Cut into squares.

Peanut mound clusters

Yield: 1½ pounds

1 cup creamy peanut butter
6 ounces unsweetened chocolate,
   grated or finely chopped
6 ounces semi-sweet chocolate,
   grated or finely chopped
½ cup flaked coconut
½ cup raisins
1½ cups salted Spanish peanuts
Flaked coconut for garnish

1 In the top of a double boiler over
simmering water, melt the peanut
butter and chocolates, stirring until
smooth. Remove from the heat and
fold in the coconut, raisins, and
peanuts.

2 Drop by tablespoonfuls onto a
waxed paper-lined baking sheet.
Immediately sprinkle coconut over
the tops. Let cool until set.

Baking notes: The candies can also
be spooned into miniature paper
candy cups instead of onto a baking
sheet.

Pecan chocolate clusters

Yield: 24 to 30 clusters

1 cup pecan halves
14 ounces caramel candies
1 tablespoon evaporated milk
2 ounces semi-sweet chocolate,
   grated or finely chopped
1 ounce milk chocolate,
   grated or finely chopped

1 Line a baking sheet with waxed
paper.

2 Arrange the pecan halves in
clusters on the prepared baking
sheet.

3 In a small saucepan, over low
heat, melt the caramels with the
evaporated milk, stirring until
smooth. Remove from the heat
and cool for 5 minutes, or until
the mixture is thick.

4 Melt the semi-sweet chocolate.
Remove from the heat and stir in
the milk chocolate, stirring until
smooth.

5 Spoon teaspoonfuls of the
caramel mixture onto each pecan
cluster. Top with a spoonful of the
melted chocolate and cool slightly.
Cover and chill until firm.

Baking notes: It may be necessary to
spread the melted chocolate over the
pecan clusters. Another method
would be to omit the semi-sweet and
milk chocolates and to chill the
caramel coated pecan clusters until
firm. Coat each cluster with dipping
chocolate (see page 126). Place the
chocolate-coated clusters on a baking sheet lined with waxed paper to
cool until set.

Scotch drops

Yield: 1½ pounds
Chill time: 1 hour

6 ounces semi-sweet chocolate,
   grated or finely chopped
1 cup butterscotch chips
1 can (7 ounces) salted peanuts,
   chopped
1 cup puffed rice cereal

1 In the top of a double boiler over
simmering water, melt the chocolate and butterscotch chips, stirring
until smooth. Stir in the peanuts
and the cereal.

2 Drop by teaspoonfuls onto a
waxed paper-lined baking sheet.
Chill for 1 hour or until solid.

**BAKING NOTES: The candy can be
spooned into miniature paper
candy cups instead of onto a
baking sheet.**

White chocolate marshmallow bars

Yield: 24 servings
Chill time: 1 hour

½ cup chopped pecans
1 tablespoon butter or margarine
1⅓ cups miniature marshmallows
8 ounces white chocolate or almond
   bark, grated or finely chopped

1 Line an 8 by 4-inch loaf pan with
waxed paper, allowing the ends of
the paper to extend over the two
long sides of the pan.

2 In a small skillet, over low heat,
sauté the pecans in the butter for 4
to 5 minutes, or until toasted, stirring constantly. Remove from the
heat.

3 Arrange half of the marshmallows
in a single layer on the bottom of
the prepared pan. Do not crowd
the marshmallows or let them
touch the sides of the pan. Press
the chopped pecans into the spaces
between the marshmallows.

4 Melt the white chocolate. Pour
over the top of the marshmallows
in the pan and spread evenly.
Gently tap the loaf pan on a flat
surface to force the white chocolate
to the bottom of the pan. Press the
remaining marshmallows evenly
into the top of the white chocolate.
Chill for 1 hour or until firm.

5 Using the ends of the waxed
paper as handles, lift the candy
from the pan. Remove the paper
and cut into 24 bars.

ALMOND BROWNIE BARS

YIELD: *2 dozen*
BAKING TIME: *50 minutes*

ALMOND-FLAVORED CHOCOLATE CHIP COOKIES WITH CREAM CHEESE ICING

YIELD: *2 to 3 dozen*
BAKING TIME: *12 minutes*

FIRST LAYER
½ cup butter or margarine,
  at room temperature
1 cup ground almonds
⅓ cup granulated sugar
1 cup all-purpose flour
SECOND LAYER
¼ cup butter or margarine
1 ounce unsweetened chocolate,
  grated or finely chopped
⅓ cup granulated sugar
1 large egg
¾ cup all-purpose flour
THIRD LAYER
1 cup almond paste
¼ cup butter or margarine,
  at room temperature
½ cup granulated sugar
2 large eggs

1 Position a rack in the center of the oven and preheat the oven to 350 degrees. Lightly grease a 9-inch square pan.

2 To make the first layer, in a large bowl, using an electric mixer on medium speed, beat the butter, almonds, sugar, and flour until a crumbly mixture forms. Press evenly onto the bottom of the prepared pan.

3 To make the second layer, in the top of a double boiler over simmering water, melt the butter and chocolate, stirring until smooth. Remove from the heat. Beat in the sugar, egg, and flour until thoroughly blended. Spread evenly over the top of the first layer.

4 To make the third layer, crumble the almond paste into a medium bowl. Using an electric mixer on high speed, beat in the butter, sugar, and eggs. Spread the mixture evenly over the top of the second layer.

5 Bake for 45 to 50 minutes, or until the edges start to pull away from the sides of the pan. The center will be firm. Cool in the pan on a wire rack. Cut into 24 bars.

COOKIES
1 cup all-purpose flour
½ cup ground almonds
½ teaspoon baking soda
¼ cup butter or margarine,
  at room temperature
¼ cup granulated sugar
¾ cup packed light-brown sugar
1 large egg
1 tablespoon amaretto
1 teaspoon almond extract
½ cup semi-sweet chocolate chips
ICING
3 cups powdered sugar
3 ounces cream cheese,
  at room temperature
4 teaspoons amaretto

1 Position a rack in the center of the oven and preheat the oven to 375 degrees. Lightly grease two baking sheets.

2 To make the cookies, combine the flour, almonds, baking soda, and salt.

3 In a large bowl, using an electric mixer on medium speed, beat the butter and sugars until smooth. Beat in the egg, amaretto, and almond extract. Gradually stir in the dry ingredients. Fold in the chocolate chips. Drop the dough by spoonfuls 1½ inches apart onto the prepared baking sheets.

4 To make the icing, combine the sugar, cream cheese, and amaretto in a medium bowl. Using an electric mixer, on medium speed, beat until smooth.

5 Bake for 10 to 12 minutes, or until a light golden brown. Transfer to a wire rack to cool. Using a pastry brush, brush with icing while cookies are still warm. Cool cookies completely and brush again with icing.

Apricot Brownies

YIELD: *2 dozen*
BAKING TIME: *15 minutes*

¼ cup dried apricots, diced
1 tablespoon apricot liqueur
4 ounces semi-sweet chocolate,
  grated or finely chopped
4 ounces unsweetened chocolate,
  grated or finely chopped
2 tablespoons butter or margarine
¼ cup all-purpose flour
¼ teaspoon baking powder
Pinch of salt
2 large eggs
¾ cup granulated sugar
1 cup pecans or hazelnuts, chopped
1 cup white chocolate chips
¼ cup flaked coconut

1 Position the rack in the center of the oven and preheat the oven to 350 degrees. Lightly grease a 13 by 9-inch pan.

2 Place the apricots in a small bowl and sprinkle with the liqueur. Soak for 10 minutes. Drain and reserve the liqueur.

3 In the top of a double boiler over simmering water, melt the chocolates and butter, stirring until smooth. Remove from the heat.

4 Combine the flour, baking powder, and salt.

5 In a large bowl, using an electric mixer on medium speed, beat the eggs until thick and light-colored. Beat in the sugar and reserved liqueur. Pouring it in a thin stream, beat in the chocolate mixture. Gradually blend in the dry ingredients. Fold in the apricots, pecans, white chocolate chips, and coconut. Pour the mixture into the prepared pan and spread evenly.

6 Bake for 12 to 15 minutes, or until a cake tester inserted into the center comes out clean. Cool in the pan on a wire rack. Cut into 24 bars.

Basic brownie master mix

YIELD: *14 cups brownie mix*
BAKING TIME: *30 minutes*

3 cups all-purpose flour
2 cups unsweetened cocoa powder
1 tablespoon baking powder
2 teaspoons salt
3½ cups vegetable shortening
  (see Baking notes)
5 cups granulated sugar

1 To make the brownie master mix: combine the flour, cocoa powder, baking powder, and salt.

2 In a large bowl, using an electric mixer on medium speed, beat the vegetable shortening and sugar until smooth. Gradually blend in the dry ingredients. Store in an air-tight container at room temperature until ready to use. This lasts for up to 1 year.

3 To make the brownies, position a rack in the center of the oven and preheat the oven to 350 degrees. Grease a 9-inch square pan.

4 Place 2¾ cups of the Basic Brownie Master Mix in a large bowl. Add 2 beaten large eggs and 1 teaspoon vanilla extract. Using an electric mixer on medium speed, beat until thoroughly mixed.

5 Pour the mixture into the prepared pan and spread evenly.

6 Bake for 25 to 30 minutes, or until a cake tester inserted into the center comes out clean. Cool in the pan on a wire rack. Cut into 12 bars.

BAKING NOTES: **This mix will make 5 single recipes as described above. The vegetable shortening must be the type that does not need refrigeration. Optional ingredients to mix in are 1 cup chopped walnuts, peanuts, or almonds; ¼ teaspoon mint extract; 1 cup semi-sweet chocolate chips, white chocolate chips, peanut butter chips, or butterscotch chips.**

Biscotti with Mascarpone

Yield: *8 servings*
Chill time: *8 hours*

3 large eggs, separated
Pinch of salt
⅔ cup powdered sugar
10 ounces mascarpone cheese
  (1¼ cups)
¼ cup dark rum
1 package (7 ounces) biscotti
⅓ cup strong brewed coffee
2 tablespoons semi-sweet chocolate,
  grated

1 In a medium bowl, using an electric mixer on medium speed, beat the egg whites and salt until stiff but not dry.

2 In a large bowl, using an electric mixer on medium speed, beat the egg yolks and powdered sugar until thick and light-colored. Add the mascarpone and rum and beat until smooth. Fold in the egg whites.

3 Arrange the biscotti on a shallow serving plate and sprinkle the coffee over the top. Spread the mascarpone mixture evenly over the biscotti. Sprinkle the chocolate over the top. Chill for 8 to 10 hours, or until serving.

Baking notes: Due to the raw eggs used in this recipe, it should be kept refrigerated at all times, and for no longer than 3 to 5 days.

Brownie Drop Cookies

Yield: *1 to 2 dozen*
Baking time: *10 minutes*

8 ounces semi-sweet chocolate,
  grated or finely chopped
¼ cup all-purpose flour
¼ teaspoon baking powder
¼ teaspoon ground cinnamon
Pinch of salt
1 tablespoon butter or margarine,
  at room temperature
¾ cup granulated sugar
2 large eggs
½ teaspoon chocolate or
  vanilla extract
¾ cup pecans, finely chopped
1 cup Chocolate Glaze IV
  (see page 123) (optional)

1 Position a rack in the center of the oven and preheat the oven to 350 degrees. Lightly grease two baking sheets.

2 Melt the chocolate. Remove from the heat.

3 Combine the flour, baking powder, cinnamon, and salt.

4 In a large bowl, using an electric mixer on medium speed, beat the butter and sugar until combined. Beat in the eggs. Beat in the chocolate extract. Gradually blend in the melted chocolate. Gradually stir in the dry ingredients. Fold in the pecans. Drop the dough by spoonfuls onto the prepared baking sheets.

5 Bake for 8 to 10 minutes, or until the cookies look dry. Transfer to wire racks to cool. Frost the cookies with chocolate glaze if desired.

BROWNIES WITH RAISINS AND MARSHMALLOWS

YIELD: *1 dozen*
BAKING TIME: *25 minutes*

½ cup all-purpose flour
½ teaspoon salt
¼ cup vegetable shortening
2 ounces semi-sweet chocolate, grated or finely chopped
1 cup granulated sugar
1 teaspoon vanilla or chocolate extract
2 large eggs
1 cup raisins (optional)
1 cup miniature marshmallows (optional)

1 Position a rack in the center of the oven and preheat the oven to 325 degrees. Lightly grease an 8-inch square pan.

2 Combine the flour and salt.

3 In a double boiler over simmering water, melt the shortening and chocolate, stirring until smooth. Remove from the heat. Using an electric mixer on medium speed, beat in the sugar and vanilla extract. On high speed, beat in the eggs. Gradually blend in the dry ingredients. Fold in the raisins and marshmallows. Pour the mixture into the prepared pan and spread evenly.

4 Bake for 20 to 25 minutes, or until a cake tester inserted into the center comes out clean. Cool in the pan on a wire rack. Cut into 12 squares.

BUTTERMILK BROWNIES

YIELD: *3 dozen*
BAKING TIME: *18 minutes*

BROWNIES
2 cups all-purpose flour
1 teaspoon baking soda
½ teaspoon salt
1 cup butter or margarine
1 cup water
⅓ cup Dutch processed cocoa powder
2 cups granulated sugar
½ cup buttermilk
2 large eggs
1 teaspoon crème de cacao

FROSTING
½ cup butter or margarine
6 tablespoons buttermilk
⅓ cup Dutch processed cocoa powder
½ cup powdered sugar

1 Position a rack in the center of the oven and preheat the oven to 350 degrees. Grease a 15½ by 10½-inch jelly-roll pan.

2 To make the brownies, in a large bowl, combine the flour, baking soda, and salt.

3 In a large saucepan, over medium heat, melt the butter. Add the water and cocoa powder, stirring until smooth. Remove from the heat and stir in the sugar until dissolved. Add the dry ingredients and mix until combined. Beat in the buttermilk, eggs, and crème de cacao. Pour the mixture into the prepared pan and spread evenly.

4 Bake for 15 to 18 minutes, or until a cake tester inserted into the center comes out clean. Cool in the pan on a wire rack.

5 To make the frosting, in a medium saucepan, over medium heat, melt the butter. Mix in the buttermilk and cocoa powder. Bring to a boil and simmer for 1 minute.

6 In a medium bowl, place the powdered sugar. Pouring it in a thin stream, beat in the cocoa mixture just until mixed. Do not overmix. Cool for 5 minutes at room temperature. Spread the frosting over the top of the brownies. Cut into 36 bars.

Chocolate almond cookies

YIELD: *2 dozen*
BAKING TIME: *20 minutes*
CHILL TIME: *50 minutes*

CRUST
1 envelope premelted unsweetened chocolate
¼ cup butter or margarine
1 large egg
½ cup granulated sugar
¼ cup all-purpose flour
¼ cup sliced almonds

FILLING
1 cup powdered sugar
2 tablespoons butter or margarine, at room temperature
1 tablespoon evaporated milk or heavy cream
¼ teaspoon almond extract

TOPPING
1 ounce semi-sweet chocolate
1 tablespoon butter or margarine

1 Position a rack in the center of the oven and preheat the oven to 350 degrees. Lightly grease an 8-inch square pan.

2 To make the crust, in the top of a double boiler over simmering water, melt the chocolate and butter, stirring until smooth. Remove from the heat.

3 In a medium bowl, using an electric mixer on medium speed, beat the egg until thick and light-colored. Beat in the chocolate mixture and sugar. Gradually blend in the flour. Fold in the almonds and mix thoroughly. Pour the mixture into the prepared pan and spread evenly.

4 Bake for 15 to 20 minutes, or until a cake tester inserted into the center comes out clean. Cool in the pan for 20 minutes.

5 To make the filling, in a small bowl, blend the powdered sugar, butter, evaporated milk, and almond extract. Spread evenly over the baked crust and chill for 30 minutes.

6 To make the topping, in the top of a double boiler over simmering water, melt the chocolate and butter, stirring until smooth. Drizzle over the top of the filling and chill for 20 minutes. Cut into 24 bars.

Chocolate and coconut tea strips

YIELD: *64 bars*
BAKING TIME: *15 minutes*

1½ cups all-purpose flour
1½ teaspoons baking powder
¼ teaspoon salt
6 tablespoons butter or margarine, at room temperature
¾ cup plus 2 tablespoons granulated sugar
1 large egg
2 tablespoons milk
½ teaspoon vanilla or chocolate extract
1 ounce unsweetened chocolate, grated or finely chopped
1 teaspoon grated orange zest
¼ cup pecans or walnuts, chopped
⅔ cup flaked coconut

1 Position a rack in the center of the oven and preheat the oven to 375 degrees. Lightly grease two 8-inch square pans.

2 Combine the flour, baking powder, and salt.

3 In a large bowl, using an electric mixer on medium speed, beat the butter and ¾ cup of the sugar until light and fluffy. Beat in the egg. Beat in the milk and vanilla extract. Gradually stir in the dry ingredients. Divide dough in half and place half in a separate bowl.

4 Melt the chocolate. Remove from the heat and mix into the dough in one bowl. On a floured surface, roll out the chocolate dough into an 8-inch square and fit into one of the prepared pans. Sprinkle with 1 tablespoon of the sugar and ½ teaspoon of the orange zest. Set aside.

5 Combine the pecans and coconut. Blend into the dough in the second bowl. On a floured surface, roll out the dough into an 8-inch square and fit into the other prepared pan. Sprinkle with the remaining 1 tablespoon sugar and ½ teaspoon orange zest.

6 Bake both pans at the same time for 10 to 15 minutes, or until a cake tester inserted into the center comes out clean. Cool in the pans on wire racks. Cut each cake into 1 by 2-inch strips.

CHOCOLATE APRICOT SPRITZ

YIELD: *20 cookies*
BAKING TIME: *12 minutes*

2 ounces unsweetened chocolate, grated or finely chopped
2¼ cups all-purpose flour
¼ teaspoon salt
¾ cup vegetable shortening
½ cup granulated sugar
1 large egg
1 teaspoon almond or hazelnut extract
½ cup apricot preserves
½ cup chopped almonds
2 tablespoons granulated sugar

1 Position a rack in the center of the oven and preheat the oven to 400 degrees.

2 Melt the chocolate. Remove from the heat.

3 Combine the flour and salt.

4 In a large bowl, using an electric mixer on medium speed, beat the shortening and sugar until fluffy. Beat in the egg and almond extract. Beat in the melted chocolate. Gradually stir in the dry ingredients.

5 Fill a pastry bag fitted with a ribbon tip with the dough. Pipe out four 12½-inch strips onto an ungreased baking sheet. Spread a thin layer of apricot preserves over each strip. Press or pipe out another strip of dough on top of the preserves.

6 Combine the almonds and sugar in a small bowl. Sprinkle evenly over the tops of the strips. Cut each strip into five pieces.

7 Bake for 10 to 12 minutes, or until a golden brown. Transfer to wire racks to cool.

BAKING NOTES: **Almost any kind of fruit preserves can be used to fill these cookies.**

CHOCOLATE BANANA RAISIN COOKIES

YIELD: *2 to 3 dozen*
BAKING TIME: *40 minutes*

6 ounces semi-sweet chocolate, grated or finely chopped
2 cups plus 2 tablespoons all-purpose flour
¼ cup Dutch processed cocoa powder
2 teaspoons baking powder
¼ teaspoon baking soda
¼ teaspoon salt
¾ cup butter or margarine, at room temperature
½ cup granulated sugar
½ cup packed light-brown sugar
1 teaspoon chocolate or vanilla extract
2 large eggs
1 cup mashed bananas (3 medium)
1½ cups chopped pecans
10 ounces white chocolate or almond bark, diced
1 cup golden raisins, chopped

1 Position a rack in the center of the oven and preheat the oven to 350 degrees. Lightly grease two baking sheets.

2 Melt the semi-sweet chocolate. Remove from the heat.

3 Combine the flour, cocoa powder, baking powder, baking soda, and salt.

4 In a large bowl, using an electric mixer on medium speed, beat the butter, sugars, and chocolate extract until fluffy. Beat in the eggs, one at a time, beating well after each addition. Beat in the mashed bananas. Beat in the melted chocolate. Gradually blend in the dry ingredients. Fold in the pecans, white chocolate, and raisins. Drop the dough by spoonfuls 1½ inches apart onto the prepared baking sheets.

5 Bake for 18 minutes. Reduce the oven temperature to 300 degrees and continue baking for 15 to 18 minutes, or until the tops spring back when gently touched. Cool on the baking sheets for 5 minutes. Transfer to wire racks to cool completely.

Chocolate Brownies

Yield: *1 dozen*
Baking time: *35 minutes*

¾ cup all-purpose flour
½ teaspoon baking powder
½ teaspoon salt
2 ounces unsweetened chocolate, grated or finely chopped
⅓ cup butter or margarine
1 cup granulated sugar
1 teaspoon vanilla or chocolate extract
2 large eggs
½ cup walnuts or pecans, chopped

1 Position a rack in the center of the oven and preheat the oven to 350 degrees. Lightly grease a 9-inch square pan.

2 Combine the flour, baking powder, and salt.

3 In the top of a double boiler over simmering water, melt the chocolate and butter, stirring until smooth. Remove from the heat.

4 Transfer the melted chocolate and butter into a large bowl. Using an electric mixer, beat in the sugar and vanilla extract. Beat in the eggs. Gradually blend in the dry ingredients. Fold in the walnuts. Pour the mixture into the prepared pan and spread evenly.

5 Bake for 30 to 35 minutes, or until a cake tester inserted into the center comes out clean. Cool in the pan on a wire rack. Cut into 12 bars.

Chocolate Butter Balls

Yield: *2 to 3 dozen*
Baking time: *20 minutes*

1 cup ground almonds
⅔ cup all-purpose flour
¼ cup Dutch processed cocoa powder
½ cup butter or margarine, at room temperature
3 tablespoons powdered sugar
Powdered sugar for rolling

1 Position a rack in the center of the oven and preheat the oven to 350 degrees.

2 Combine the almonds, flour and cocoa powder.

3 In a medium bowl, using an electric mixer on medium speed, beat the butter and the 3 tablespoons of powdered sugar. Gradually blend in the dry ingredients. The dough will be stiff. Pinch off pieces of the dough, roll into balls, and place 1 inch apart on an ungreased baking sheet.

4 Bake for 15 to 20 minutes, or until light golden brown. Roll the hot cookies in powdered sugar and transfer to a wire rack to cool. When completely cool, roll in the powdered sugar again.

CHOCOLATE CARAMEL BARS

YIELD: *2 dozen*
BAKING TIME: *20 minutes*

CRUST
2 cups all-purpose flour
1 cup packed light-brown sugar
½ cup butter or margarine
1 cup pecans or almonds,
   finely ground
FILLING
1 cup butter or margarine
¾ cup packed light-brown sugar
TOPPING
2 cups semi-sweet chocolate chips

1 Position a rack in the center of
the oven and preheat the oven to
350 degrees. Lightly grease a 13 by
9-inch pan.

2 To make the crust, in a large
bowl, combine the flour and brown
sugar. Using a pastry blender, cut
in the butter, until the mixture
forms coarse crumbs. Press onto
the bottom of the prepared pan.
Sprinkle the pecans evenly over
the top.

3 To make the filling, in a
saucepan, over medium heat, combine the butter and brown sugar.
Stirring constantly, bring to a boil
and cook for 1 minute. Spread
evenly over the crust in the pan.

4 Bake for 15 to 20 minutes, or
until the surface is bubbly. Sprinkle
the chocolate chips over the top.
Let stand for 3 minutes. Spread the
melted chocolate chips evenly over
the top. Cool in the pan on a wire
rack. Cut into 24 bars.

BAKING NOTES: White chocolate chips
can also be used.

CHOCOLATE CHARLIES

YIELD: *12 to 14 dozen*
BAKING TIME: *12 minutes*
CHILL TIME: *2 hours*

3¼ cups all-purpose flour
¼ cup Dutch processed cocoa powder
1 teaspoon baking soda
¼ teaspoon ground cinnamon
½ teaspoon salt
1 cup vegetable shortening
1½ cups packed light-brown sugar
2 large eggs
1 cup crème de cacao
Semi-sweet chocolate chips for
   garnish

1 Position a rack in the center of
the oven and preheat the oven to
350 degrees. Lightly grease two
baking sheets.

2 Combine the flour, cocoa powder,
baking soda, cinnamon, and salt.

3 In a large bowl, using an electric
mixer on medium speed, beat the
shortening and brown sugar until
fluffy. Beat in the eggs. Gradually
blend in the dry ingredients, alternating with the crème de cacao.
Cover and chill for at least 2 hours.

4 Fill a pastry bag fitted with a
large star tip with the dough. Pipe
out stars onto the prepared baking
sheets, spacing them 1 inch apart.
Place a single chocolate chip into
the center of each star.

5 Bake for 10 to 12 minutes, or
until a golden brown. Transfer to
wire racks to cool.

BAKING NOTES: Chilling the dough
keeps the stars from spreading out
while baking. White chocolate chips
can be used in place of the semi-
sweet chocolate chips. The dough
can also be dropped by teaspoonfuls
instead of using a pastry bag.

CHOCOLATE CHEWS

YIELD: *2 dozen*
BAKING TIME: *40 minutes*

CHOCOLATE CHIP MANDELS

YIELD: *3 to 4 dozen*
BAKING TIME: *30 minutes*

½ cup vegetable shortening
2 ounces unsweetened chocolate, grated or finely chopped
2 large eggs
1 cup granulated sugar
½ teaspoon almond or hazelnut extract
½ cup all-purpose flour
1 cup slivered almonds

1 Position a rack in the center of the oven and preheat the oven to 350 degrees. Lightly grease a 13 by 9-inch pan.

2 In the top of a double boiler over simmering water, melt the shortening and chocolate, stirring until smooth. Remove from the heat.

3 Transfer the melted chocolate and shortening into a large bowl. Using an electric mixer on medium speed, beat in the eggs, one at a time, beating well after each addition. Beat in the sugar and almond extract. Blend in the flour. Pour the mixture into the prepared pan and spread evenly. Sprinkle the slivered almonds over the top.

4 Bake for 35 to 40 minutes, or until a cake tester inserted into the center comes out clean. Cool in the pan on a wire rack. Cut into 24 bars.

3 cups all-purpose flour
3 tablespoons Dutch processed cocoa powder
2 teaspoons baking powder
¼ teaspoon salt
3 large eggs
1 cup canola oil
1 cup granulated sugar
2 cups semi-sweet chocolate chips

1 Position a rack in the center of the oven and preheat the oven to 350 degrees. Lightly grease a baking sheet.

2 Combine the flour, cocoa powder, baking powder, and salt.

3 In a large bowl, using an electric mixer on medium, beat the eggs until thick and light-colored. Beat in the canola oil. Beat in the sugar. Gradually stir in the dry ingredients. Fold in the chocolate chips.

4 Divide the dough in half and form each half into a log 3 inches in diameter. Place the logs 1½ inches apart on the prepared baking sheet.

5 Bake for 30 minutes, or until a cake tester inserted into the center comes out clean. Cool on the baking sheet for 10 minutes. Cut each log in half lengthwise and cut each half into 1-inch slices. Transfer to wire racks to cool completely.

Chocolate chip peanut logs

Yield: *2 dozen*
Chill time: *30 minutes*

1 cup semi-sweet chocolate chips
½ cup creamy peanut butter
½ cup peanuts, chopped (optional)
4 cups rice crispy cereal

1 Lightly grease a 9-inch square pan.

2 In the top of a double boiler over simmering water, melt the chocolate chips and peanut butter. Remove from the heat. Blend in the chopped peanuts. Gradually blend in the cereal. Be sure the cereal is well coated with the chocolate mixture.

3 Pour the mixture into the prepared pan and spread evenly. Cool in the pan on a wire rack until the mixture hardens slightly. Chill for 30 minutes in the refrigerator.

4 Cut into 24 bars. Roll the bars between your palms to form logs. Wrap individually in waxed paper or plastic wrap and store tightly covered until serving.

Baking notes: This is a great recipe to make with children. Let them roll the logs.

Chocolate christmas cookies

Yield: *2 to 3 dozen*
Baking time: *10 minutes*

1 cup all-purpose flour
1 cup whole wheat flour
½ cup soy flour
1 cup Dutch processed cocoa powder
½ teaspoon baking soda
1 teaspoon ground allspice
Pinch of salt
1 cup butter or margarine, at room temperature
2 cups granulated sugar
1 teaspoon chocolate or vanilla extract
1 large egg
1 tablespoon crème de cacao
Cocoa Sugar for garnish (see page 125)

1 Position a rack in the center of the oven and preheat the oven to 400 degrees. Lightly grease two baking sheets.

2 Combine the flours, cocoa powder, baking soda, allspice, and salt.

3 In a large bowl, using an electric mixer on medium speed, beat the butter, sugar, and chocolate extract until light and fluffy. Beat in the egg and crème de cacao. Gradually stir in the dry ingredients.

4 On a floured surface, knead the dough until smooth. Roll out the dough to a thickness of ⅛ to ¼ inch. Using a 2-inch round cookie cutter or floured glass, cut the dough into rounds. Place 1 inch apart on the prepared baking sheets. Sprinkle the tops with cocoa sugar.

5 Bake for 8 to 10 minutes, or until the cookies look very dry. Do not overbake. Transfer to wire racks to cool.

Baking notes: This recipe can be used to make sandwich cookies. Fill the cookies with Coffee Mocha Icing (see page 126).

CHOCOLATE COATED MACAROONS

YIELD: *2 to 3 dozen*
BAKING TIME: *25 minutes*
CHILL TIME: *70 minutes*

MACAROONS
4 large egg whites
1⅓ cups granulated sugar
1½ teaspoons almond extract
¼ teaspoon salt
2½ cups flaked coconut
6 tablespoons all-purpose flour
COATING
4 ounces unsweetened chocolate,
   grated or finely chopped
4 ounces semi-sweet chocolate,
   grated or finely chopped

1 Position a rack in the center of the oven and preheat the oven to 300 degrees. Lightly grease two baking sheets.

2 To make the macaroons, in a saucepan, combine the egg whites, sugar, almond extract, and salt and stir until thoroughly blended. Blend in the coconut and flour. Place over medium heat and cook, stirring constantly, for 5 minutes. Raise the heat to medium-high and cook, stirring constantly, for 4 minutes, or until the mixture is thick and pulls away from the sides of the pan. Immediately transfer to a large bowl and cool for 5 minutes. Cover and chill for at least 10 minutes, or until the dough is cold.

3 Drop the dough by teaspoonfuls 1½ inches apart onto the prepared baking sheets.

4 Bake for 20 to 25 minutes, or until a light golden brown. Transfer to wire racks to cool completely.

5 To make the coating, in the top of a double boiler over simmering water, melt the chocolates, stirring constantly until smooth. Remove from the heat.

6 Line a baking sheet with waxed paper. Dip the macaroons into the chocolate, coating half of each cookie. Place on the prepared baking sheet. Chill for 30 minutes. When the chocolate has hardened, coat the other half with chocolate and place on the pan to harden. Chill for 30 minutes.

BAKING NOTES: **Do not use a skewer to dip the cookies. They will fall off into the chocolate while dipping.**

Chocolate coconut toffee bars

YIELD: *8 to 10 servings*
BAKING TIME: *30 minutes*

1¼ cups all-purpose flour
⅓ cup Dutch processed cocoa powder
¾ cup butter-flavored vegetable shortening
1 cup powdered sugar
2 tablespoons butter or margarine
1 can (14 ounces) sweetened condensed milk
2 teaspoons chocolate or almond extract
1 cup semi-sweet chocolate chips
½ cup flaked coconut

1 Position a rack in the center of the oven and preheat the oven to 350 degrees. Lightly grease a 13 by 9-inch pan.

2 Combine the flour and cocoa powder.

3 In a large bowl, using an electric mixer on medium speed, beat the shortening and sugar until fluffy. Gradually blend in the dry ingredients. Pour mixture into the prepared pan and spread evenly.

4 Bake for 15 minutes.

5 In the top of a double boiler over simmering water, melt the butter with the milk until thickened. (It will take about 15 minutes.) Remove from the heat and stir in the chocolate extract. Immediately pour this over the baked crust.

6 Bake for 10 minutes, or until a cake tester inserted into the center comes out clean.

7 Sprinkle the chocolate chips evenly over the top and bake for 3 to 5 minutes, or until the chocolate is melted. Remove from the oven. Using a knife, spread the melted chocolate chips over the top. Sprinkle with the coconut. Cool in the pan on a wire rack. Cut into bars.

Chocolate cookie kisses I

YIELD: *2 to 3 dozen*
BAKING TIME: *40 minutes*

2 ounces unsweetened chocolate, grated or finely chopped
4 large egg whites
¼ teaspoon salt
¼ teaspoon cream of tartar
1 cup granulated sugar
¼ teaspoon almond extract

1 Position a rack in the center of the oven and preheat the oven to 250 degrees. Line two baking sheets with wax or parchment paper.

2 Melt the chocolate. Remove from the heat.

3 In a large bowl, using an electric mixer on high speed, beat the egg whites until foamy. Beat in the sugar. Mix in the salt and cream of tartar. Add the almond extract and beat until the mixture forms stiff peaks. Fold in the melted chocolate. Drop the mixture by spoonfuls 1 inch apart onto the prepared baking sheets.

4 Bake for 35 to 40 minutes, or until firm to the touch. Transfer to wire racks to cool.

BAKING NOTES: For crisper kisses, turn the oven off after baking and leave the baking sheet in the oven until the cookies are cool. (Do not open the oven door.)

Chocolate Cornucopias

Yield: *1½ to 2 dozen*
Baking time: *10 minutes*

COOKIES
1 cup semi-sweet chocolate chips
½ cup vegetable shortening
½ cup granulated sugar
Pinch of salt
¼ teaspoon ground ginger
⅓ cup light corn syrup
1 cup plus 2 tablespoons
    all-purpose flour

FILLING
8 ounces cream cheese,
    at room temperature
2 cups heavy cream
½ teaspoon chocolate or
    vanilla extract
2 ounces semi-sweet chocolate,
    grated or finely chopped

1 Position a rack in the center of the oven and preheat the oven to 350 degrees. Grease two baking sheets.

2 To make the cookies, in the top of a double boiler over simmering water, melt the chocolate chips, stirring until smooth. Stir in shortening, sugar, salt, and ginger until smooth. Remove from the heat. Using a wooden spoon, blend in the corn syrup and flour. Drop by tablespoonfuls 3 inches apart onto the prepared baking sheets.

3 To make the filling, using an electric mixer on medium speed, beat the cream cheese until very soft. Add the cream and chocolate extract. Whip on high speed until soft peaks form. Fold in the grated chocolate.

4 Bake for 8 to 10 minutes, or until dry-looking. Cool on the baking sheet for 1 to 2 minutes. Remove the cookies and shape into cornucopia cone by using a cone mold or roll into cones. Lay on a wire rack to cool completely, seam-side down.

5 When the cookies are cool, fill a pastry bag with a medium star tip. Pipe the filling into the cookies.

Chocolate Covered Oatmeal Cookies

Yield: *3 to 4 dozen*
Baking time: *15 minutes*

2½ cups old-fashioned oats
1¼ cups all-purpose flour
1 teaspoon baking soda
½ teaspoon salt
½ cup butter or margarine,
    at room temperature
½ cup chunky peanut butter
1 cup granulated sugar
1 cup packed light-brown sugar
2 large eggs
¼ cup milk
1 teaspoon almond extract
3 ounces semi-sweet chocolate,
    grated or finely chopped
½ cup golden raisins
1 recipe Dipping Chocolate
    (see page 126)

1 Position a rack in the center of the oven and preheat the oven to 350 degrees.

2 Combine the oats, flour, baking soda, and salt.

3 In a large bowl, using an electric mixer on medium speed, beat the butter, peanut butter, and sugars until smooth. Beat in the eggs, one at a time, beating well after each addition. Beat in the milk and almond extract. Gradually stir in the dry ingredients. Fold in the chocolate and raisins. Drop the dough by tablespoonfuls 2½ to 3 inches apart onto ungreased baking sheets.

4 Bake for 12 to 15 minutes, or until dry-looking. Transfer to wire racks to cool.

5 Make the dipping chocolate.

6 When completely cooled, place the cookies on wire racks set over a baking sheet. Spoon the dipping chocolate over the tops of the cookies, letting the excess chocolate drip off. When the chocolate is firm enough to handle, transfer the coated cookies to a piece of waxed paper to harden.

Chocolate Cream Dream Bars

Yield: *3 dozen*
Baking time: *30 minutes*

Chocolate Crinkles

Yield: *3 to 4 dozen*
Baking time: *15 minutes*

CRUST
2½ cups all-purpose flour
2 cups old-fashioned oats
1½ cups packed light-brown sugar
1 teaspoon baking soda
¼ teaspoon salt
1 cup butter-flavored vegetable shortening or margarine

FILLING
2 cups semi-sweet chocolate chips
1 can (14 ounces) sweetened condensed milk
2 tablespoons butter-flavored vegetable shortening or margarine
2 teaspoons chocolate or vanilla extract
1 cup pecans, finely chopped (optional)

1 Position a rack in the center of the oven and preheat the oven to 350 degrees.

2 To make the crust, in a large bowl, combine the flour, oats, brown sugar, baking soda, and salt. Using a pastry blender, cut in the shortening to make a crumbly mixture. Press 4 cups onto the bottom of an ungreased 15½ by 10½-inch jelly-roll pan. Reserve the remaining crust mixture.

3 To make the filling, in the top of a double boiler over simmering water, melt the chocolate chips, stirring until smooth. Add the condensed milk and shortening and heat thoroughly. Remove from the heat and stir in the chocolate extract and pecans. Immediately pour over the crust in the pan. Sprinkle with the reserved crust mixture.

4 Bake for 25 to 30 minutes, or until a cake tester inserted into the center comes out clean. Cool in the pan on a wire rack. Cut into 36 bars.

BAKING NOTES: **For a festive occasion, spread chocolate whipped cream (see page 125) over the bars before serving.**

2 cups all-purpose flour
2 teaspoons baking powder
3 ounces semi-sweet chocolate, grated or finely chopped
½ cup canola oil
1½ cups granulated sugar
1 teaspoon vanilla or chocolate extract
2 large eggs
¼ cup milk
Powdered sugar for rolling

1 Position a rack in the center of the oven and preheat the oven to 350 degrees. Lightly grease two baking sheets.

2 Combine the flour and baking powder.

3 Melt the chocolate. Remove from the heat.

4 In a large bowl, using an electric mixer on medium speed, beat the oil, sugar, and vanilla extract until smooth. Beat in the eggs, one at a time, beating well after each addition. Beat in the melted chocolate. Beat in the milk. Gradually stir in the dry ingredients.

5 Pinch off walnut-sized pieces of the dough and roll into balls. Roll each ball in powdered sugar and place 1½ inches apart on the prepared baking pans.

6 Bake for 12 to 15 minutes, or until firm to the touch. Roll in powdered sugar again while still warm. Transfer to wire racks to cool.

Chocolate DELIGHT BARS

YIELD: *1 dozen*
BAKING TIME: *40 minutes*

Chocolate DIPPED HEALTH FOOD COOKIES I

YIELD: *2 dozen*
CHILL TIME: *30 minutes*

CRUST
½ cup butter or margarine,
   at room temperature
3 tablespoons powdered sugar
2 large eggs yolks
   (reserve the whites for topping)
1 teaspoon instant coffee powder
1 tablespoon warm water
2 cups all-purpose flour

TOPPING
½ cup semi-sweet chocolate chips
2 large egg whites
¼ granulated sugar
¼ cup almonds, finely ground
¼ cup almonds, chopped,
   for garnish

1 Position a rack in the center of the oven and preheat the oven to 350 degrees. Lightly grease a 9-inch square pan.

2 In a large bowl, using an electric mixer on medium speed, beat the butter, powdered sugar, egg yolks, coffee powder, and water until smooth. Gradually blend in the flour. The mixture will be crumbly. Pour the mixture into the prepared pan and spread evenly.

3 Bake for 20 minutes. Remove from the oven. While the crust is baking, make the topping.

4 To make the topping, melt the chocolate. Remove from the heat.

5 In a medium bowl, using an electric mixer on high speed, beat the egg whites until foamy. Beat in the granulated sugar and beat until stiff peaks form. Pouring it in a steady stream, beat in the melted chocolate. Fold in the ground almonds.

6 Spread the topping mixture over the hot crust, sprinkle with the chopped almonds, and bake for 20 minutes longer, or until a cake tester inserted into the center comes out clean. Cool in the pan on a wire rack. Cut into 12 bars.

3 cups granola
½ cup raisins
½ cup chopped unsalted peanuts
½ cup flaked coconut
¾ cup chunky peanut butter
½ cup light corn syrup
½ cup honey
1 recipe Dipping Chocolate
   (see page 126)

1 Lightly grease a 13 by 9-inch baking pan.

2 In a large bowl, combine the granola, raisins, peanuts, and coconut.

3 In a saucepan, over medium heat, combine the peanut butter, corn syrup, and honey. Bring to a boil and cook for 1 minute. Remove from the heat. Add to the dry ingredients. Using a wooden spoon, stir until everything is well coated. Pour the mixture into the prepared pan and spread evenly. Chill for 30 minutes. Cut into 24 bars.

4 Make the dipping chocolate.

5 Dip the bars into the chocolate, coating half of each bar. Place on a sheet of waxed paper to set. When the chocolate has hardened, dip the other half in the chocolate and place on the waxed paper to set. Individually wrap the bars in waxed paper or plastic wrap and chill until serving.

CHOCOLATE FILLED CUSHIONS

Yield: *2 to 3 dozen*
Baking time: *15 minutes*

CUSHIONS
3 cups all-purpose flour
¼ teaspoon salt
1 cup butter or margarine, at room temperature
1 cup packed light-brown sugar
2 teaspoons chocolate or vanilla extract
1½ tablespoons milk
½ cup Hershey's™ semi-sweet chocolate candy bar sprinkles
Powdered sugar for rolling

FILLING
1¾ cups semi-sweet chocolate chips
2 tablespoons vegetable shortening
¼ cup light corn syrup
2 tablespoons crème de cacao
1 teaspoon chocolate or vanilla extract

1 Position a rack in the center of the oven and preheat the oven to 350 degrees.

2 To make the cushions, combine the flour and salt.

3 In a large bowl, using an electric mixer on medium speed, beat the butter, brown sugar, and chocolate extract until blended. Stir in the milk. Gradually stir in the dry ingredients. Fold in the chocolate sprinkles. Pinch off 1-inch pieces of the dough and roll into balls. Place the balls 1 inch apart on ungreased baking sheets. Press your thumb into the center of each ball to make a deep indentation.

4 To make the filling, in the top of a double boiler over simmering water, melt the chocolate chips and shortening, stirring until smooth. Stir in the corn syrup and chocolate extract and cook, stirring constantly, for 5 minutes. Do not let the mixture boil. Remove from the heat.

5 Bake for 12 to 15 minutes, or until a light golden brown. Roll the hot cookies in powdered sugar. Spoon ½ teaspoon into the indentation in each cookie. Place on the wire rack and let cool until the filling has set.

CHOCOLATE-FILLED OATMEAL BARS

YIELD: *3 dozen*
BAKING TIME: *15 minutes*

CRUST

3 cups quick-cooking oats
2½ cups all-purpose flour
1 teaspoon baking soda
¼ teaspoon salt
1½ cups peanuts or almonds,
  chopped
1 cup butter-flavored vegetable
  shortening
2 cups packed light-brown sugar
2 large eggs
1 tablespoon coffee liqueur
½ teaspoon instant coffee powder

FILLING

½ cup butter-flavored vegetable
  shortening
2/3 cup Dutch processed cocoa
  powder
½ cup granulated sugar
1 can (14 ounces) sweetened
  condensed milk
1½ teaspoons chocolate or vanilla
  extract

1 Position a rack in the center of the oven and preheat the oven to 350 degrees. Lightly grease a 15½ by 10½-inch jelly-roll pan.

2 To make the crust, combine the oats, flour, baking soda, salt, and pecans.

3 In a large bowl, using an electric mixer on medium speed, beat the shortening and brown sugar until fluffy. Beat in the eggs, liqueur, and coffee powder. Gradually blend in the dry ingredients. The dough will be very stiff. Spread 2 cups of the crust mixture evenly onto the bottom of the prepared pan. Reserve the remaining crust mixture.

4 To make the filling, in a large saucepan, over low heat, melt the shortening. Stir in the cocoa powder and sugar. Blend in the condensed milk and cook, stirring frequently, until the mixture is smooth and very thick. Remove from the heat and beat in the chocolate extract.

5 Spread the filling evenly over the crust in the pan. Sprinkle the reserved crust mixture over the top.

6 Bake for 20 to 25 minutes, or until the top is dull and slightly browned. Cool in the pan on a wire rack. Cut into 36 bars.

BAKING NOTES: After the remaining crust mixture is sprinkled over the top, it can be pressed down or left loose.

Chocolate Fudge Cheesecake Bars

Yield: *2 dozen*
Baking time: *25 minutes*
Chill time: *30 minutes*

4 ounces unsweetened chocolate,
  grated or finely chopped
1 cup butter or margarine
4 large eggs
2 cups granulated sugar
1 teaspoon almond or chocolate
  extract
8 ounces cream cheese, at room
  temperature
2 cups all-purpose flour

1 Position a rack in the center of the oven and preheat the oven to 350 degrees. Lightly grease a 13 by 9-inch pan.

2 In the top of a double boiler over simmering water, melt the chocolate and butter, stirring until smooth. Remove from the heat.

3 In a medium bowl, using an electric mixer on medium speed, beat the eggs until thick and light-colored. Beat in the sugar and almond extract just until blended. On low speed, beat in the chocolate mixture, pouring it in a thin stream. Blend in the cream cheese. Gradually blend in the flour. Pour the mixture into the prepared pan and spread evenly.

4 Bake for 20 to 25 minutes, or until dough pulls away from the sides of the pan. Cool in the pan on a wire rack. Chill for about 30 minutes. Cut into 24 bars.

Chocolate Marble Bars

Yield: *1 dozen*
Baking time: *45 minutes*

CREAM CHEESE BATTER
6 ounces cream cheese,
  at room temperature
2 tablespoons butter or margarine,
  at room temperature
¼ cup granulated sugar
2 tablespoons cornstarch
2 large eggs
½ teaspoon grated lemon zest

CHOCOLATE BATTER
2 ounces semi-sweet chocolate,
  grated or finely chopped
¾ cup all-purpose flour
¾ cup granulated sugar
½ teaspoon baking soda
½ teaspoon salt
⅓ cup buttermilk
¼ cup butter or margarine,
  at room temperature
1 large egg
½ teaspoon chocolate or vanilla extract

1 Position a rack in the center of the oven and preheat the oven to 350 degrees. Lightly grease a 9-inch square pan.

2 To make the cream cheese batter, in a large bowl, using an electric mixer on medium speed, beat the cream cheese and butter until blended. Beat in the sugar and cornstarch until smooth. Beat in the eggs, one at a time, beating well after each addition. Beat in the lemon zest. Pour the mixture into the prepared pan and spread evenly.

3 To make the chocolate batter, melt the chocolate. Remove from the heat.

4 In a large mixing bowl, combine the flour, sugar, baking soda, and salt. Using an electric mixer on medium speed, beat in the buttermilk, butter, and melted chocolate until blended. Beat on medium speed for 2 to 3 minutes. Beat in the egg and chocolate extract. Spoon the mixture evenly over the top of the cream mixture already in the baking pan. Using a knife, gently swirl the two mixtures together. Do not overmix.

5 Bake for 40 to 45 minutes, or until a cake tester inserted into the center comes out clean. Cool in the pan on a wire rack. Cut into 12 bars.

CHOCOLATE MINT BARS WITH ALMONDS

YIELD: *2 dozen*
BAKING TIME: *15 minutes*

2 cups all-purpose flour
½ teaspoon baking powder
½ cup slivered almonds
1 cup mint chocolate chips
8 ounces cream cheese,
    at room temperature
¾ cup butter or margarine,
    at room temperature
¾ cup granulated sugar
1 teaspoon vanilla or
    chocolate extract
1 cup semi-sweet chocolate chips
    for garnish
½ cup chopped almonds for garnish

1 Position a rack in the center of the oven and preheat the oven to 375 degrees. Grease a 13 by 9-inch pan.

2 Combine the flour, baking powder, almonds, and mint chocolate chips.

3 In a large bowl, using an electric mixer on medium speed, beat the cream cheese, butter, and sugar until blended. Beat in the vanilla extract. Gradually stir in the dry ingredients. Pour the mixture into the prepared pan and spread evenly.

4 Bake for 12 to 15 minutes, or until a cake tester inserted into the center comes out clean. Sprinkle the chocolate chips over the top. Let stand for 3 minutes. Spread the melted chocolate chips evenly over the top. Sprinkle with the chopped almonds and cool completely on a wire rack. Cut into 24 bars.

CHOCOLATE SANDWICH COOKIES

YIELD: *2 to 3 dozen*
BAKING TIME: *12 minutes*
CHILL TIME: *overnight*

2 cups all-purpose flour
¼ teaspoon baking soda
¼ teaspoon allspice
¼ teaspoon salt
½ cup butter or margarine,
    at room temperature
⅔ cup packed light-brown sugar
1 large egg
½ teaspoon chocolate or vanilla
    extract
1 cup semi-sweet chocolate chips
    for filling

1 Combine the flour, baking soda, allspice, and salt.

2 In a large bowl, using an electric mixer on medium speed, beat the butter and brown sugar until smooth. Beat in the egg and chocolate extract. Gradually stir in the dry ingredients. The dough will be stiff. Form the dough into a log 3 inches in diameter. Wrap with waxed paper and chill overnight.

3 Position a rack in the center of the oven and preheat the oven to 350 degrees.

4 Cut the chilled log into ⅛-inch slices. Place the slices ¾ inch apart on an ungreased baking sheet.

5 Bake for 10 to 12 minutes, or until lightly colored. Transfer to wire rack to cool.

6 Melt the chocolate chips. Place the cookies bottom-side up, and spread a thin layer of the melted chocolate on half of the cookies. Top with the remaining cookies bottom side down, to form sandwich cookies.

CREAM CHEESE MARBLED BROWNIES

YIELD: *2 dozen*
BAKING TIME: *75 minutes*
CHILL TIME: *overnight*

CAKE
1½ cups all-purpose flour
1½ teaspoons baking powder
¼ teaspoon salt
12 ounces semi-sweet chocolate, grated or finely chopped
1 cup butter or margarine
5 large eggs
1 cup granulated sugar
1¼ cups packed light-brown sugar
1 tablespoon almond or chocolate extract
2 cups chopped almonds

FILLING
12 ounces cream cheese, at room temperature
5 tablespoons butter or margarine, at room temperature
¾ cup granulated sugar
1½ teaspoons almond or chocolate extract
3 large eggs

1 Position a rack in the center of the oven and preheat the oven to 350 degrees. Lightly grease and flour a 13 by 9-inch pan.

2 To make the cake, combine the flour, baking powder, and salt.

3 In the top of a double boiler over simmering water, melt the chocolate and the butter, stirring until smooth. Remove from the heat.

4 In a large bowl, using an electric mixer on medium speed, beat the eggs just until foamy. Add the sugars and almond extract, beating just until mixed. Beat in the almonds. Beat in the melted chocolate. Gradually blend in the dry ingredients, mixing just until blended. Reserve 2¼ cups of the batter. Pour the remaining mixture into the pan and spread evenly.

5 To make the filling, in a small bowl, using an electric mixer on medium speed, beat the cream cheese and butter until smooth. Beat in the sugar and almond extract. Beat in the eggs, one at a time, beating well after each addition. Slowly pour the filling over the chocolate mixture in the pan.

6 Pour the reserved chocolate mixture slowly to cover all of the filling. Be sure the filling mixture is totally covered at the sides of the pan. Using a knife, sweep through the mixture to create a marbleized effect. Do not overmix.

7 Bake for 60 to 75 minutes, or until a cake tester inserted into the center comes out clean. Do not overbake. Cool in the pan on a wire rack for 10 minutes. Invert onto a platter, cover with waxed paper, and chill overnight. Cut into 24 bars.

BAKING NOTES: Frost the chilled brownies with ½ cup Chocolate Glaze IV (see page 123), if desired.

CRÈME DE MENTHE SQUARES

Yield: 12 to 16 squares
Chill time: 30 minutes

BOTTOM LAYER
½ cup butter or margarine
½ cup Dutch processed cocoa powder
½ cup powdered sugar
1 large egg, beaten
1 teaspoon white crème de menthe
2 cups graham cracker crumbs

MIDDLE LAYER
½ cup butter or margarine
⅓ cup green crème de menthe
3 cups powdered sugar

TOP LAYER
¼ cup butter or margarine
1½ cups semi-sweet chocolate chips

1 To make the bottom layer, in a medium saucepan, over low heat, melt the butter. Add the cocoa powder, stirring until smooth. Remove from the heat and add the powdered sugar, egg, and white crème de menthe. Stir in the graham cracker crumbs. Pour the mixture into the bottom of an ungreased 13 by 9-inch pan and spread evenly.

2 To make the middle layer, in a medium saucepan, over low heat, melt the butter. Remove from the heat and stir in the green crème de menthe. Gradually blend in the powdered sugar. Spread evenly over the bottom layer in the pan.

3 To make the top layer, in the top of a double boiler over simmering water, melt the butter and chocolate chips, stirring until smooth. Spread this mixture evenly over the middle layer. Chill for 30 minutes, or until firm. Cut into 12 to 16 bars.

BAKING NOTES: Due to the raw egg used in this recipe, it should be kept refrigerated at all times, and for no longer than 3 days.

CHOCOLATE
CHIFFON PIE

YIELD: *8 to 10 servings*
CHILL TIME: *2 ½ hours*

1 recipe Chocolate Pastry Crust (see page 124)

FILLING
¼ cup plus 5 tablespoons milk
1 envelope unflavored gelatin
1 large egg
2 tablespoons granulated sugar
4 ounces semi-sweet chocolate, grated or finely chopped
¼ teaspoon peppermint extract
½ cup heavy cream
¾ cup crushed ice

TOPPING
3 tablespoons powdered sugar
2 tablespoons Dutch processed cocoa powder
1 cup heavy cream
½ teaspoon crème de cacao
Chocolate Leaves (see page 128) for garnish
Fresh mint leaves for garnish

1 Make and bake the pie crust.

2 To make the filling, in a cup, sprinkle the gelatin over ¼ cup of the milk. Let stand for 1 minutes to soften.

3 In a small saucepan, heat the remaining 5 tablespoons of milk just until simmering. Remove from the heat, add the gelatin mixture, and stir constantly until the gelatin no longer clings to the sides of the pan. Transfer to a medium bowl. Add the egg, sugar, and chocolate, and using an electric mixer on high speed, beat for 3 to 4 minutes, or until very smooth. Beating constantly, add the peppermint extract, cream, and crushed ice. Beat on high speed until the ice is completely melted. Pour the mixture into the

prepared pie crust and chill for at least 2 hours, or until the filling is set.

4 To make the topping, combine the powdered sugar and cocoa powder.

5 In a medium bowl, using an electric mixer on high speed, whip the cream until soft peaks form. Fold in the sugar and cocoa. Fold in the crème de cacao. Chill for 30 minutes. Spread the topping over the filling.

6 Just before serving, arrange the mint leaves and chocolate leaves in a decorative arrangement over the pie.

BAKING NOTES: To keep the pie crust from becoming soggy, sprinkle chocolate cookie crumbs in the bottom of the pipe crust before adding the filling.

Chocolate
COFFEE CREAM PIE
YIELD: *8 to 10 servings*
CHILL TIME: *30 minutes*

CRUST
**1 recipe Chocolate Pastry Crust
(see page 124)**

FILLING
**2 cups milk
2 ounces unsweetened chocolate,
grated or finely chopped
¼ cup granulated sugar
¼ cup cornstarch
4 large egg yolks
3 tablespoons butter or margarine
1 tablespoon coffee liqueur
1 tablespoon cream sherry
1 recipe Chocolate Whipped Cream
(see page 125) for garnish**

1 Make and bake the pie crust.

2 To make the filling, in the top of
a double boiler over simmering
water, heat the milk and chocolate,
stirring until the chocolate is melted and the mixture is smooth.

3 In a large bowl, using an electric
mixer on medium speed, beat the
sugar, cornstarch, and egg yolks
until well blended. On low speed,
pouring it in a thin stream, beat in
1 cup of the hot milk mixture.

4 Pour the egg mixture into the
milk mixture in the double boiler
and cook, stirring constantly, until
thickened. Stir in the butter until
melted. Remove from the heat and
stir in the liqueur and sherry. Pour
mixture into the prepared pie crust.
Chill for 30 minutes, or until firm.

5 Make Choclate Whipped Cream,
and spread over chilled pie just
before serving.

Chocolate
ICE CREAM CAKE II
YIELD: *8 to 10 servings*
FREEZING TIME: *4 hours*

**3 cups chocolate wafer cookie
crumbs
½ cup chopped pecans
1 cup semi-sweet chocolate chips
½ cup butter or margarine, melted
1 pint chocolate ice cream, softened
1 pint vanilla ice cream, softened
1 pint heavy cream
Ground pecans for garnish**

1 In a large bowl, blend the cookie
crumbs, pecans, chocolate chips,
and melted butter. Pour one-third of
this mixture into the bottom of a
9-inch springform pan and spread
evenly.

2 Spread the chocolate ice cream
over the crumb mixture and top
with half of the remaining crumb
mixture. Spread with the vanilla
ice cream and top with the remaining crumbs. Cover and freeze for
4 hours.

3 In a medium bowl, using an
electric mixture on high, whip the
cream until soft peaks form.

4 To assemble, remove the side of
the pan and transfer the cake to a
serving plate. Frost the top and
sides with whipped cream and
sprinkle with the pecans.

**BAKING NOTES: For a variation, use
lime or raspberry sherbet in place of
the vanilla ice cream.**

CHOCOLATE ICE CREAM PIE

YIELD: *8 to 10 servings*
BAKING TIME: *1 hour*
CHILL/FREEZING TIME: *9 hours*

MERINGUE CRUST
¾ cup granulated sugar
2 tablespoons Dutch processed cocoa powder
3 large egg whites
¼ teaspoon cream of tartar
Pinch of salt

CHOCOLATE FILLING
1 package (3.4 ounces) Jell-O Brand chocolate instant pudding mix
¼ cup milk
1 pint chocolate ice cream, softened
½ cup heavy cream
Sliced fresh fruit for garnish

1 Position a rack in the center of the oven and preheat the oven to 275 degrees. Lightly grease a 9-inch pie pan.

2 To make the crust, combine the sugar and cocoa powder.

3 In a medium bowl, using an electric mixer on high speed, beat the egg whites, cream of tartar, and salt until foamy. Sprinkle the sugar and cocoa powder over the top and beat until stiff but not dry. Pour the mixture evenly over the bottom and sides of the prepared pan.

4 Bake for 1 hour. Cool in the pan on a wire rack.

5 To make the filling, in a medium bowl, using an electric mixer on medium speed, beat the pudding mix and milk. Add the softened ice cream and beat for 2 minutes. Pour the mixture into the cooled shell and freeze for at least 8 hours.

6 In a small bowl, using an electric mixer on high speed, whip the cream until stiff peaks form. Spread over the top of the pie and freeze for 1 hour. When ready to serve, arrange the sliced fruit over the top of the whipped cream.

CHOCOLATE MARSHMALLOW FREEZE

YIELD: *1 pint*
CHILL TIME: *1 hour*

1 can (14 ounces) evaporated milk
⅓ cup Dutch processed cocoa powder
¼ cup granulated sugar
¼ cup marshmallow creme
Chocolate Sauce V (see page 124) for serving

1 Measure and reserve ½ cup of the evaporated milk. Place the remaining evaporated milk in a medium bowl and place in the freezer until ready to whip.

2 In a medium saucepan, over low heat, combine the cocoa powder and sugar, stirring until smooth and the sugar is dissolved. Stir in the reserved evaporated milk. Add the marshmallow creme and cook until blended. Remove from the heat and set the pan in a large bowl of ice and water. Stir until completely cool.

3 Using an electric mixer on high speed, beat the chilled evaporated milk until stiff peaks form. Fold in the cocoa mixture and pour into a 9-inch square pan. Cover and freeze for 1 hour, or until firm. Serve with chocolate sauce on the side.

CHOCOLATE MINT CREAM PIE

YIELD: *8 to 10 servings*
FREEZING TIME: *1 hour*

COOKIE CRUMB CRUST
1¼ cups chocolate wafer cookie crumbs
¼ cup finely ground hazelnuts
3 tablespoons granulated sugar
6 tablespoons butter or margarine, melted

CHOCOLATE AND VANILLA FILLINGS
1 quart vanilla ice cream, softened
2 tablespoons white crème de menthe
1½ quarts chocolate ice cream, softened

CHOCOLATE TOPPING
1 cup Chocolate Sauce VIII (see page 125)
Fresh mint sprigs for garnish

1 To make the crust, in a medium bowl, combine the cookie crumbs, hazelnuts, and sugar. Using a fork, blend in the melted butter. Press the mixture evenly onto the bottom and sides of a 9-inch pie pan. Cover with waxed paper and weigh down with dried beans or uncooked rice. Freeze until ready for use.

2 Line a medium bowl (see Baking notes) with plastic wrap, allowing it to hang over the edges.

3 In a medium bowl, using an electric mixer on low speed, combine the vanilla ice cream and crème de menthe. Pour the mixture into the prepared bowl. Cover and freeze for 1 hour, or until firm.

4 Spread the chocolate ice cream evenly over the chilled crust and freeze until firm.

5 Make the chocolate sauce.

6 To assemble, using the edges of the plastic wrap as handles, remove the vanilla ice cream from the bowl. Invert on top of the chocolate ice cream in the pie pan. Remove the plastic wrap. Pour the sauce over the top of the mound of vanilla ice cream and allow the excess to drip down and puddle around the base. Garnish with mint sprigs.

BAKING NOTES: Be sure the diameter of the bowl used to mold the vanilla ice cream is at least 1 inch less than that of the pie plate. This will allow for 1 inch of free space for the chocolate sauce to puddle in.

CHOCOLATE MINT ICE CREAM PIE I

YIELD: *8 to 10 servings*
FREEZING TIME: *1 hour*

1 recipe Chocolate Cookie Crumb Crust (see page 122)
1 quart chocolate mint ice cream, softened
1 cup miniature chocolate chips
2 cups Chocolate Fudge Sauce (see page 123)
1 cup Chocolate Syrup I (see page 125) for garnish
1 cup heavy cream

1 Make and bake the pie crust.

2 Spread half of the ice cream over the baked and cooled pie crust. Sprinkle the chocolate chips on the top. Spread the remaining ice cream over the top. Cover and freeze 1 hour, or until firm.

3 Make the fudge sauce and chocolate syrup.

4 In a medium bowl, using an electric mixer on high speed, whip the cream until soft peaks form.

5 To serve, spread the fudge sauce over the pie. Spread the whipped cream over the sauce. Drizzle with the chocolate syrup.

CHOCOLATE MOUSSE PIE

YIELD: *8 to 10 servings*
CHILL TIME: *2 hours*

1 recipe Chocolate Pastry Crust (see page 124)
1½ teaspoons unflavored gelatin
1 tablespoon cold water
2 tablespoons boiling water
½ cup plus 1 tablespoon granulated sugar
1¼ cups heavy cream
⅓ cup Dutch processed cocoa powder
1 teaspoon chocolate extract
Chocolate Cutouts (see page 122) for garnish

1 Make and bake the pie crust.

2 To make the filling, in a cup, sprinkle the gelatin over the cold water. Let stand for 2 minutes to soften. Add the boiling water and stir until the gelatin is completely dissolved.

3 In the top of a double boiler over simmering water, combine ½ cup of the sugar, ½ cup of the cream, the cocoa powder, and chocolate extract. Using an electric mixer on medium speed, beat until the mixture thickens. Remove from the heat and beat in the gelatin mixture. Pour the mixture into the prepared pastry crust and chill for 2 hours.

4 To serve, in a large bowl, using an electric mixer on high speed, whip the remaining ¾ cup cream and 1 tablespoon sugar until soft peaks form. Spread over the top of the pie. Garnish with chocolate cutouts.

Chocolate
MOUSSE TARTS

Yield: *12 servings*
Baking time: *12 minutes*
Chill time: *30 minutes*

CHOCOLATE CRUST
2 ounces semi-sweet chocolate,
    grated or finely chopped
1 cup all-purpose flour
¼ teaspoon salt
3 tablespoons water
CHOCOLATE CUSTARD
FILLING
2 large eggs, separated
1 tablespoon unflavored gelatin
1 cup milk
6 ounces semi-sweet chocolate,
    grated or finely chopped
1 cup granulated sugar
1 teaspoon chocolate or
    vanilla extract
2 tablespoons powdered sugar
TOPPING
1 cup heavy cream
¼ cup granulated sugar
1 teaspoon crème de cacao
Chocolate wafer cookies for garnish

1 Position a rack in the center of
the oven and preheat the oven to
400 degrees. Lightly grease twelve
3-inch muffin pan cups.

2 To make the crust, melt the
chocolate. Remove from the heat.

3 In a medium bowl, combine the
flour and salt. Stir in the melted
chocolate. Sprinkle the water over
the top. Gently stir with a fork
until the dough holds together.

4 On a lightly floured surface, roll
out the dough to a thickness of ¼
to ½ inch and cut into twelve 5-
inch rounds. Press the rounds into
the prepared muffin cups and flute
the edges.

5 Bake for 10 to 12 minutes. Cool
completely in the pan on a wire rack.

6 To make the filling, in a small
bowl, using an electric mixer on
medium speed, beat the egg yolks
until thick and light-colored.

7 In a cup, sprinkle the gelatin
over the milk. Let stand for 1 minutes to soften.

8 In the top of a double boiler over
simmering water, melt the chocolate, stirring until smooth. Add the
milk mixture and stir until smooth
and the gelatin is completely dissolved. Add the granulated sugar
and chocolate extract, stirring until
blended. Stir in the beaten egg yolks.
Cook, stirring constantly, until the
mixture just starts to thicken. Remove
from the heat and beat until slightly set. Cool.

9 In a medium bowl, using an
electric mixer on high speed, beat
the egg whites until stiff but not
dry. Fold in the powdered sugar.
Fold the egg whites into the chocolate mixture. Cover and chill 30
minutes, just until set.

10 To make the topping, in a medium bowl, using an electric mixer
on high speed, whip the cream
until soft peaks form. Fold in the
sugar and crème de cacao.

11 To serve, remove the tart shells
from the pan. Fill each tart with the
custard mixture and top with the
whipped cream. Garnish with a
wedge of chocolate wafer cookie.

Chocolate peanut
BUTTER PIE II

Yield: *8 to 10 servings*
Chill time: *30 minutes*

CRUST
1 recipe Chocolate Cookie Crumb Crust (see page 122)

PEANUT BUTTER LAYER
½ **cup creamy peanut butter**
¼ **cup butter or margarine, at room temperature**
1½ **cups powdered sugar**

CHOCOLATE LAYER
2⅓ **cups milk**
2 **tablespoons arrowroot or cornstarch**
1½ **ounces unsweetened chocolate, grated or finely chopped**
1 **tablespoon butter or margarine**
3 **large egg yolks**
1 **cup granulated sugar**
½ **teaspoon chocolate or vanilla extract**
½ **cup heavy cream for topping**

1 Make and bake the pie crust.

2 To make the peanut butter layer, in a medium bowl, using an electric mixer on medium speed, beat the peanut butter and butter until smooth. Gradually beat in the powdered sugar until blended. Pour the mixture into the prepared pie crust and spread evenly.

3 To make the chocolate layer, in a cup, combine ⅓ cup of the milk and the arrowroot.

4 In the top of a double boiler over simmering water, melt the chocolate and butter, stirring until smooth. Stir in the remaining 2 cups milk and stir until smooth. Remove from the heat.

5 In a medium bowl, using an electric mixer on medium speed, beat the egg yolks and sugar until combined. Beat in the arrowroot mixture. Beating continually on low speed, mix in the chocolate

mixture. Pour into the saucepan and return to the heat. Cook, stirring constantly in slow circles, until the mixture thickens. Remove from the heat and stir in the chocolate extract. Cool. Pour the mixture into the prepared crust and chill for 30 minutes, or until set.

6 In a medium bowl, using an electric mixer on high speed, whip the cream until soft peaks form. Spread over the top of the chilled pie.

Chocolate
PECAN PIE I

YIELD: *8 to 10 servings*
BAKING TIME: *1 hour*

CRUST
1 recipe Low-fat Pastry Shell (see page 127)

FILLING
1½ cups pecans, chopped
1 cup unsweetened chocolate chips
2 large eggs
½ cup light corn syrup
½ cup granulated sugar
¼ cup butter or margarine, melted
Chocolate Whipped Cream (see page 125) for garnish

1 Make and bake the pie crust. Bake for only 3 to 4 minutes.

2 Sprinkle the pecans and chocolate chips over the bottom of the prepared crust.

3 In a medium bowl, using an electric mixer on medium speed, beat the eggs, corn syrup, and sugar until smooth. Beat in the melted butter until blended. Pour the mixture into the prepared crust and spread evenly.

4 Bake for 60 minutes, or until a cake tester is inserted into the center comes out clean. Cool on a wire rack for 10 minutes.

5 Make the chocolate whipped cream. Spread over the top of the pie before serving.

BAKING NOTES: Coconut Pie Crust (see page 125) can be substituted for the low-fat pie crust.

Everyman's FAVORITE PIE

YIELD: *8 to 10 servings*
FREEZING TIME: *1 hour*

CHOCOLATE TOPPING
2 ounces unsweetened chocolate,
   grated or finely chopped
2 ounces semi-sweet chocolate,
   grated or finely chopped
⅔ cup water
1 cup granulated sugar
6 tablespoons butter or margarine, at
   room temperature
1 teaspoon chocolate extract or crème
   de cacao
CRUST
1 recipe Chocolate Pastry Crust (see
   page 124)
ICE CREAM FILLINGS
1 pint chocolate ice cream, softened
1 pint vanilla ice cream, softened
MERINGUE TOPPING
3 large egg whites
⅛ teaspoon cream of tartar
½ cup granulated sugar

1 To make the chocolate topping,
in the top of a double boiler over
simmering water, melt the chocolates with the water, stirring until
smooth. Add the sugar and stir
until dissolved. Remove from the
heat and immediately stir in the
butter and chocolate extract until
blended. Transfer to a medium
bowl. Cover and chill while making the crust.

2 Make and bake the pie crust.

3 To assemble the pie, spread the
vanilla ice cream in the prepared
pie crust. Spread ½ cup of the topping over the top of the ice cream.
Freeze for 30 minutes.

4 Spread the chocolate ice cream
over the top of the sauce and top
with another ½ cup of the sauce.
Freeze for 30 minutes.

5 To make the meringue topping,
in a medium bowl, using an electric mixer on high speed, beat the
egg whites and cream of tartar
until foamy. Add the sugar and
beat until stiff and glossy. Spread
the meringue over the top of the
frozen pie so that it touches the
edges of the crust.

6 Bake in a 400-degree oven for 1
to 2 minutes, or until the meringue
is browned. Serve at once with the
remaining chocolate topping as a
sauce on the side.

**BAKING NOTES: Due to the raw egg
whites, keep this pie in the freezer at
all times, up to two weeks.**

FRENCH SILK PIE

YIELD: *8 to 10 servings*
BAKING TIME: *15 to 20 minutes*
CHILL TIME: *2 hours*

PASTRY CRUST
2 cups all-purpose flour
½ teaspoon salt
⅔ cup butter-flavored vegetable shortening
5 to 6 tablespoons ice water

CHOCOLATE SILK FILLING
2 ounces unsweetened chocolate, grated or finely chopped
½ cup butter or margarine, at room temperature
¾ cup granulated sugar
2 large eggs
1 teaspoon crème de cacao
Chocolate Whipped Cream (see page 125) for garnish

1 Position a rack in the center of the oven and preheat the oven to 375 degrees.

2 To make the crust, combine the flour and salt. Using a pastry blender or two knives scissor fashion, cut in the shortening until the mixture forms fine crumbs. Sprinkle the water over the top, a little at a time, and mix gently with a fork just until the dough is moist enough to hold together. Form into a ball. Wrap and chill for 1 hour, or until firm.

3 On a lightly floured surface, roll the dough out into a circle about ¼ inch thick. Press the mixture firmly into the bottom and sides of a 9-inch pie pan. Trim the edges and flute if desired. Line the crust with a piece of aluminum foil and fill with dried beans or pie weights.

4 Bake for 15 to 20 minutes, or until the edges of the crust are golden brown. Remove the foil and beans. Cool completely on a wire rack.

5 To make the filling, melt the chocolate. Transfer to a medium bowl. Using an electric mixer on low speed, beat in the butter and sugar. On medium speed, beat in the eggs, one at a time, mixing for 5 minutes after each addition. Beat in the crème de cacao. Pour the mixture into the prepared crust and chill for 1 hour or until set. Garnish each serving with a dab of chocolate whipped cream.

BAKING NOTES: **Due to the raw eggs used in this recipe, it should be kept refrigerated at all times, and for no longer than 3 days.**

FROZEN CHOCOLATE ICE CREAM PIE

YIELD: *8 to 10 servings*
FREEZING TIME: *1 hour*

CHOCOLATE GRAHAM CRACKER CRUST
¼ cup butter-flavored vegetable shortening
2 ounces unsweetened chocolate, grated or finely chopped
1 teaspoon coffee liqueur
1 cup chocolate graham cracker crumbs
¼ cup powdered sugar

CHOCOLATE ICE CREAM
3 ounces unsweetened chocolate, grated or finely chopped
3 ounces semi-sweet chocolate, grated or finely chopped
2 tablespoons boiling water
½ cup granulated sugar
¼ cup water
½ teaspoon cream of tartar
Pinch of salt
4 large egg yolks
3 cups heavy cream
1 tablespoon chocolate or vanilla extract
Chocolate Whipped Cream (see page 125) for garnish Chocolate Curls (see page 122) for garnish

1 Position a rack in the center of the oven and preheat the oven to 350 degrees. Lightly grease a 9-inch pie pan.

2 To make the crust, in the top of a double boiler over simmering water, melt the shortening and chocolate, stirring until smooth. Remove from the heat. Stir in the liqueur.

3 In a large bowl, combine the crumbs and sugar. Mix in the chocolate mixture. Press the mixture firmly into the bottom and sides of the prepared pan.

4 Bake for 10 minutes. Cool completely on a wire rack. Chill while preparing the ice cream.

5 To make the ice cream, in the top of a double boiler over simmering water, melt the chocolates and the 2 tablespoons boiling water, stirring until the chocolate is melted and smooth. Remove from the heat.

6 In a small saucepan, over medium heat, combine the sugar, ¼ cup water, cream of tartar, and salt. Bring to a boil. Insert a candy thermometer and cook, without stirring, until 238 degrees.

7 In a large bowl, using an electric mixer on medium speed, beat the egg yolks until thick and light-colored. Beating constantly on low speed, pour in the syrup in a thin stream. Beat in the chocolate mixture. Beat in the cream and chocolate extract. Pour into a freezer-safe glass bowl and freeze for 30 minutes, or until almost firm, stirring several times.

8 Spread the ice cream over the chilled pie crust. Garnish with chocolate whipped cream and chocolate curls. Freeze until the ice cream is hard before serving.

Frozen chocolate parfaits

Yield: *8 servings*
freezing time: *8 hours*

**CHOCOLATE AND
COFFEE CUSTARDS**
⅔ cup granulated sugar
⅓ cup water
3 large egg yolks
4 ounces unsweetened chocolate,
  grated or finely chopped
4 teaspoons instant coffee powder
1 tablespoon coffee liqueur
1⅓ cups heavy cream

WHIPPED CREAM TOPPING
½ cup heavy cream
2 tablespoons granulated sugar
Chocolate coffee bean candies for
  garnish

1 To make the custard, in a saucepan, over low heat, stir the sugar and water until the sugar is completely dissolved. Insert a candy thermometer and increase the heat to medium. Bring to a boil and simmer, without stirring, for about 5 minutes, until 245 degrees.

2 In a medium bowl, using an electric mixer on medium speed, beat the egg yolks until thick and light-colored. Pouring it in a thin stream, gradually beat in the hot syrup and beat for about 5 minutes, until the mixture is cool. Pour one-third of the yolk mixture into a small bowl.

3 Melt the chocolate. Remove from the heat and immediately beat into the medium bowl with the remaining two-thirds of the yolk mixture.

4 Dissolve the coffee powder in the liqueur and beat into the egg yolk mixture poured into the small bowl.

5 In another medium bowl, using an electric mixer on high speed, whip the cream until soft peaks form. Fold two-thirds of the whipped cream into the chocolate mixture. Fold the remaining whipped cream into the coffee mixture.

6 Spoon half of the chocolate mixture into eight parfait glasses. Spoon all of the coffee mixture over the top of the chocolate mixture in the glasses. Top with the remaining chocolate mixture. Cover with plastic wrap and freeze for at least 8 hours.

7 To make the topping, in a small bowl, using an electric mixer on high speed, beat the cream and sugar until soft peaks form. Chill until ready to use.

8 One hour before serving, remove the parfaits from the freezer. Remove the plastic wrap and top each with a dab of whipped cream. Garnish with chocolate coffee beans.

BAKING NOTES: The chocolate coffee beans can also be crushed and sprinkled over the top of the whipped cream.

FUDGE PECAN PIE

YIELD: *8 to 10 servings*
BAKING TIME: *40 minutes*

1 recipe Chocolate Pastry Crust (see page 124)
4 ounces semi-sweet chocolate, grated or finely chopped
¼ cup butter-flavored vegetable shortening
1 can (14 ounces) sweetened condensed milk
2 large eggs
¼ cup hot water
1 teaspoon almond extract
Pinch of salt
½ cup pecan pieces
Dessert Syrup (see page 126) for garnish

1 Position a rack in the center of the oven and preheat the oven to 400 degrees.

2 Make and bake the pie crust. Cool in a wire rack. Reduce the oven temperature to 350 degrees.

3 To make the filling, in the top of a double boiler over simmering water, melt the chocolate and shortening, stirring until smooth. Remove from the heat.

4 In a large bowl, using an electric mixer on medium speed, beat the condensed milk, eggs, hot water, almond extract, and salt until well blended. Beat in the chocolate mixture. Pour the mixture into the prepared crust and top with the pecan pieces.

5 Bake for 35 to 40 minutes, or until a cake tester inserted into the center comes out clean. Cool on a wire rack. Lightly brush the dessert syrup over the top of the pecans.

LUSCIOUS CHOCOLATE ALMOND PIE

YIELD: *8 to 10 servings*
BAKING TIME: *9 hours*

ALMOND CRUST
1 cup all-purpose flour
1 cup chopped almonds
1 cup butter or margarine, softened

FLUFFY CREAM CHEESE FILLING
8 ounces cream cheese, at room temperature
1 cup powdered sugar
1 cup whipped topping

CHOCOLATE PUDDING FILLING
2 packages (3.4 ounces each) Jell-O Brand chocolate instant pudding mix
2 cups cold milk
1½ cups whipped topping for garnish
½ cup chopped almonds for garnish

1 Position a rack in the center of the oven and preheat the oven to 325 degrees.

2 To make the crust, in a medium bowl, combine the flour and almonds. Using a pastry blender or two knives scissor fashion, cut the butter into the flour. Press the mixture firmly onto the bottom and sides of a 9-inch glass pie plate.

3 Bake for 20 minutes. Cool completely on a wire rack.

4 To make the cream cheese filling, in a large bowl, using an electric mixer on medium speed, beat the cream cheese until smooth. Beat in the powdered sugar until smooth. On low speed, beat in the whipped topping. Spread evenly over the baked crust.

5 To make the chocolate filling, in a small bowl, using an electric mixer on high speed, beat the pudding mix and milk. Spread over the cream cheese filling. Chill for 1 hour. Fill a pastry bag fitted with a large star tip with the whipped topping and pipe rosettes over the entire surface of the chilled pie. Chill for at least 8 hours before serving. Sprinkle with the chopped almonds.

Meringue tarts with chocolate filling

Yield: *8 to 10 servings*
baking time: *85 minutes*
standing time: *8 hours*

MERINGUE TART SHELLS
4 large egg whites
½ teaspoon cream of tartar
1 cup powdered sugar

CHOCOLATE MOUSSE FILLING
6 ounces semi-sweet chocolate, grated or finely chopped
4 large egg yolks
2 tablespoons heavy cream
Chocolate Curls (see page 122) for garnish
Fresh mint sprigs for garnish

1 Position a rack in the center of the oven and preheat the oven to 200 degrees. Line a baking sheet with wax or parchment paper.

2 To make the tart shells, in a large bowl, using an electric mixer on high speed, beat the egg whites and cream of tartar until foamy. Beat in the powdered sugar, a few teaspoonfuls at a time, until the sugar is dissolved. Beat until soft peaks form.

3 Using a ⅓ measuring cup, drop the mixture onto the prepared pan, 1½ inches apart. Using the back of a spoon dipped in powdered sugar, spread into a nest-shaped 3-inch circle, making a depressing in the center of each round.

4 Bake for 85 minutes. Turn off the oven and leave the tart shells in the oven for at least 8 hours.

5 To make the filling, melt the chocolate. Remove from the heat.

6 In a medium bowl, using an electric mixer on medium speed, beat the egg yolks and 2 tablespoons cream until thickened. Gradually beat in the melted chocolate. Chill until ready to fill the tarts.

7 To assemble, fill a pastry bag fitted with a large star tip with the filling. Pipe the filling into the meringue tart shells. Garnish each with chocolate curls and a small sprig of mint.

Baking notes: The meringue tarts can be frozen up to 1 week before using. Place in a zip-lock plastic bag, removing as much excess air as possible, and freeze until ready to use. For chocolate tart shells, add ⅓ of the Dutch processed cocoa powder and reduce the powdered sugar to ¾ cup. Due to the raw egg yolks used in this chocolate mousse recipe, it should be kept refrigerated at all times, and for no longer than 3 days.

Hot fudge
SUNDAE PIE I

YIELD: *8 to 10 servings*
FREEZING TIME: *1½ hours*

Chocolate Cookie Crumb Crust (see page 122)
Hot Fudge Sauce IV (see page 127)
1 quart strawberry ice cream, softened
1 quart chocolate ice cream, frozen
½ cup heavy cream

GARNISH
Maraschino cherries
Chocolate leaves (see page 128)
Chopped almonds

1 Make and bake the pie crust and make the hot fudge sauce.

2 To assemble, spread half of the strawberry ice cream over the crust and freeze for 30 minutes. Drizzle half of the fudge sauce over the top and spread with the remaining strawberry ice cream. Freeze for 30 minutes.

3 Using a small ice cream scoop, arrange balls of the chocolate ice cream over the top of the strawberry layer. Drizzle the remaining fudge sauce over the top.

4 In a medium bowl, using an electric mixture on high speed, whip the cream until soft peaks form.

5 Fill a pastry bag fitted with a large star tip with the whipped cream. Pipe rosettes around the chocolate ice cream. Freeze for 30 minutes before serving. Garnish with the cherries and chocolate leaves. Sprinkle the almonds over the top.

Hot fudge
SUNDAE PIE II
Yield: *8 to 10 servings*
Freezing time: *1 hour*

CRUST
1 recipe Chocolate Hazelnut Crumb
   Crust (see page 123)

CHOCOLATE SAUCE
1 cup granulated sugar
¾ cup Dutch processed cocoa powder
1 teaspoon instant espresso powder
1 cup heavy cream
¼ cup butter or margarine

ICE CREAM FILLING
1 quart chocolate ice cream, softened
1 quart chocolate chocolate chip ice
   cream, softened
½ cup heavy cream
2 tablespoons granulated sugar
½ cup chopped walnuts for garnish
¾ cup diced fresh cherries or
   strawberries or whole raspberries
   for garnish

1 Make and bake the pie crust.

2 To make the sauce, in a saucepan,
over low heat, combine the sugar,
cocoa powder and espresso powder. Add ½ cup of the cream and
stir to make a smooth paste. Stir in
the remaining ½ cup cream and
cook, stirring constantly, until
smooth. Stir in the butter and cook
for 4 to 6 minutes, or until the butter is melted and the mixture is
smooth. Remove from the heat.

3 To assemble the pie, spread half
of the chocolate ice cream over the
prepared crust. Carefully spoon
about half of the warm sauce over
the top. Spread the remaining
chocolate ice cream over the top of
the sauce. Freeze for 1 hour, or
until firm.

4 Using a small ice cream scoop,
place balls of the chocolate chocolate chip ice cream in a decorative
manner over the surface of the pie.
Drizzle the remaining sauce over
the top.

5 In a small bowl, using an electric
mixer on high speed, whip the
cream and sugar until stiff peaks
form. Fill a pastry bag fitted with a
large star tip with the whipped
cream. Pipe large and small
rosettes into the areas not filled
with ice cream. Sprinkle with walnuts. Freeze until ready to serve.
Garnish with the fresh fruit just
before serving.

BAKING NOTES: Almost any combination of ice cream flavors can be used
in this recipe.

Mocha fudge pie with chocolate filling

Yield: *8 to 10 servings*
baking time: *40 minutes*

MOCHA CRUST
1¼ cups all-purpose flour
⅓ cup Dutch processed cocoa powder
¼ cup granulated sugar
Pinch of salt
¾ cup butter or margarine
¼ cup cold strong brewed coffee
¼ cup coffee liqueur

MOCHA WALNUT FILLING
6 ounces semi-sweet chocolate, grated or finely chopped
6 ounces unsweetened chocolate, grated or finely chopped
2 tablespoons butter or margarine
⅔ cup granulated sugar
2 tablespoons buttermilk
2 teaspoons coffee liqueur
½ cup ground walnuts
2 large eggs
Chocolate ice cream for serving

1 Position a rack in the center of the oven and preheat the oven to 350 degrees.

2 To make the crust, in a large bowl, combine the flour, cocoa powder, sugar, and salt. Using a pastry blender or two knives scissor fashion, cut in the butter to make a crumbly mixture. Stir in the coffee. If the mixture seems dry, add the liqueur, a tablespoon at a time. Press the mixture firmly into the bottom and sides of a 9-inch pie pan. Freeze until ready to fill.

3 To make the filling, in the top of a double boiler over simmering water, melt the chocolates and butter, stirring constantly until smooth. Remove from the heat. Stir in the sugar, buttermilk, liqueur, walnuts, and eggs and blend thoroughly. Pour into the prepared pie crust.

4 Bake for 35 to 40 minutes, or until a cake tester inserted into the center comes out clean. Cool completely on a wire rack. Serve with a scoop of chocolate ice cream on the side.

Orange cream pie with chocolate shell

YIELD: *6 to 8 servings*
CHILL TIME: *3 ½ hours*
STANDING TIME: *1 hour*

1 recipe Chocolate Pie Shell (see page 124)
FILLING
1 envelope unflavored gelatin
¼ cup water
4 large eggs, separated
½ cup granulated sugar
½ cup fresh orange juice, strained
1 tablespoon grated orange zest
Pinch of salt
1 cup heavy cream
2 tablespoons Triple Sec or Curaçao

1 Make and bake the pie crust. Chill until ready to fill.

2 To make the filling, in a cup, sprinkle the gelatin over the water. Let stand for 1 minute to soften.

3 In a large bowl, using an electric mixer on medium speed, beat the egg yolks until thick and light-colored. Add ¼ cup of the sugar and beat until creamy. Add the orange juice, orange zest, and salt. Pour the mixture into the top of a double boiler over simmering water. Cook, stirring constantly, until the mixture is thick and smooth. Stir in the gelatin until dissolved. Remove from the heat and cool.

4 In a large bowl, using an electric mixer on high speed, beat the egg whites and salt until stiff but not dry. Fold in the remaining ¼ cup sugar. Fold the egg whites into the egg yolk mixture.

5 In a small bowl, using an electric mixer on high speed, beat the cream until thick. Fold in the Triple Sec. Fold the cream mixture into the egg mixture. Chill for 20 to 30 minutes, or until thickened.

6 To assemble, carefully spread the chilled custard mixture in the prepared crust and chill for at least 1 hour, or until firm.

7 To serve, let stand at room temperature for 1 hour before cutting to allow the shell to soften.

RASPBERRY ICE CREAM PIE

YIELD: *8 to 10 servings*
FREEZING TIME: *1 hour*

**CHOCOLATE COOKIE
CRUMB CRUST**
**6 tablespoons butter or margarine, at
 room temperature**
**1½ cups chocolate wafer cookie
 crumbs**
2 drops peppermint extract

ICE CREAM FILLING
1 quart vanilla ice cream, softened
**1½ quarts raspberry ice cream,
 softened**

CHOCOLATE TOPPING
½ cup granulated sugar
1 tablespoon cornstarch or arrowroot
¼ cup milk
¼ cup heavy cream
6 tablespoons butter or margarine
**3 ounces unsweetened chocolate,
 grated or finely chopped**
1 teaspoon crème de cacao

1 Position a rack in the center of
the oven and preheat the oven to
350 degrees.

2 To make the crust, in a medium
bowl, using a pastry blender or
two knives scissor fashion, cut the
butter into the cookie crumbs to
form a crumbly mixture. Stir in the
extract. Press the mixture into the bottom and sides of a 9-inch pie pan.

3 Bake for 10 minutes. Cool slightly
on a wire rack. Freeze until ready
to use.

4 To make the filling, line a large
bowl with plastic wrap. Scoop the
vanilla ice cream into the bowl,
packing it firmly. Cover and freeze
for 1 hour, or until firm.

5 Spread the raspberry ice cream
evenly over the chilled pie crust
and freeze.

6 To make the topping, in the top
of a double boiler over simmering
water, combine the sugar and cornstarch. Stir in the milk, cream, butter, and chocolate. Stir over low
heat until the chocolate is melted
and the mixture thickens. Remove
from the heat. Stir in the crème de
cacao and cool to room temperature.

7 To assemble, using the edges of
the plastic wrap as handles, lift the
vanilla ice cream out of the bowl.
Invert on top of the raspberry ice
cream. Press down slightly.
Remove the plastic wrap. Pour the
topping over the mound of vanilla
ice cream, allowing it to drip down
the sides. Serve immediately.

**BAKING NOTES: The pie will keep in
the freezer for up to 2 months.**

Scotch chocolate cream pie

Yield: *8 to 10 servings*
freeze time: *30 minutes*

Chocolate Hazelnut Crumb Crust
(see page 123)
2 cups heavy cream
3 ounces semi-sweet chocolate,
grated or finely chopped
1 ounce unsweetened chocolate,
grated or finely chopped
1 cup clover honey
⅓ cup Scotch whisky
1 cup chocolate wafer cookie crumbs
for topping
Mint sprigs for garnish
Peeled and thinly sliced kiwifruit for
garnish

1 Make and bake the pie crust.
Press the mixture firmly into the
bottom of an 8 or 9-inch springform pan. Freeze 30 minutes, or
until ready to fill.

2 In a medium bowl, using an
electric mixer on high speed, beat
the cream until soft peaks form.

3 In the top of a double boiler over
simmering water, melt the chocolates, stirring until smooth. Remove
from the heat. Stir in the honey.
Beat in the Scotch and ⅓ cup of the
whipped cream.

4 Fold the chocolate mixture into
the remaining whipped cream.
Pour the mixture into the prepared
crust and smooth the top. Sprinkle
the crushed cookie crumbs evenly
over the top. Press the crumbs very
lightly into the filling. Freeze until
the filling is set. To serve, remove
the pie from the springform pan
and cut into wedges.

Speckled chocolate pie

Yield: *8 to 10 servings*
baking time: *1 hour*

1 recipe Coconut Pie Crust
(see page 125)
2 large eggs
½ cup all-purpose flour
½ cup granulated sugar
½ cup packed light-brown sugar
1 cup butter or margarine, at room
temperature
1 cup chocolate sprinkles
1 cup pecans, chopped

1 Make and bake the pie crust.

2 To make the filling, in a large
bowl, using an electric mixer on
medium speed, beat the eggs until
thick and light-colored. Beat on
low speed and add the flour and
sugars. Beat in the butter. Fold in
the sprinkles and pecans. Pour the
mixture into the prepared crust.

3 Bake for 1 hour, or until a cake
tester inserted into the center
comes out clean. Cool completely
on a wire rack.

White
CHOCOLATE PIE

YIELD: *8 to 10 servings*
FREEZING TIME: *5 hours*

1 recipe Almond Crust (see page 121)
10 ounces white chocolate, grated or
   finely chopped
⅓ cup evaporated milk
3 tablespoons butter-flavored
   vegetable shortening
3 tablespoons crème de cacao
1½ teaspoons white chocolate liqueur
   or vanilla extract
½ teaspoon almond extract
2 large egg whites
2 tablespoons granulated sugar
1¼ cups heavy cream
1¼ cups frozen raspberries, thawed
   and drained
Whipped cream for garnish
Chocolate Leaves (see page 128)
   for garnish

1 Make and bake the pie crust.

2 To make the filling, in the top of
a double boiler over simmering
water, melt the chocolate with the
evaporated milk and shortening,
stirring until smooth. Remove from
the heat and immediately set the
pan in a bowl filled with water and
ice. Cool, stirring occasionally,
until thickened. Stir in the crème
de cacao, white chocolate liqueur,
and almond extract.

3 In a small bowl, using an electric
mixer on high speed, beat the egg
whites until foamy. Add the sugar
and continue beating until stiff
peaks form.

4 In a large bowl, using an electric
mixer on high speed, whip the cream
until stiff peaks form. Pouring it in
a thin stream, beat in the chocolate
mixture on low speed. Fold in the
egg whites. Pour the mixture into
the prepared crust and freeze for
4 to 5 hours, or until frozen. Remove
the pie from the freezer 30 minutes
before the serving.

5 To serve, mound the raspberries
in the center of the pie. Garnish
with daps of whipped cream and
the chocolate leaves.

**BAKING NOTES: Due to the raw egg
whites used in this recipe, after first
serving keep frozen at all times.**

Amaretto
CHOCOLATE PUDDING

Yield: *4 to 6 servings*
Chill time: *2 hours*

1 package (3.4 ounces) Jell-O Brand
  chocolate instant pudding mix
2 ounces semi-sweet chocolate,
  grated or finely chopped
1½ cups milk
2 tablespoons buttermilk
7 tablespoons amaretto
½ cup heavy cream
1 tablespoon granulated sugar
Sliced fresh peeled kiwifruit or
  strawberries for garnish
Macaroons for serving

1 In a medium saucepan, over low
heat, combine the pudding mix,
chocolate, milk, buttermilk and 6
tablespoons of the amaretto and
stir constantly until the chocolate is
melted and the mixture is smooth.
Raise the heat to medium and
cook, stirring constantly, until the
mixture boils and thickens. Pour
the mixture into four to six custard
cups or ramekins.

2 In a medium bowl, using an
electric mixer on high speed, beat
the cream with the sugar and
remaining 1 tablespoon amaretto
until soft peaks form. Chill until
ready to use.

3 To serve, place a dab of whipped
cream on top of each cup of pudding
and garnish with fresh fruit. Serve
with macaroons on the side.

AUSTRIAN CHOCOLATE CREAM

YIELD: *8 to 10 servings*
CHILL TIME: *5 hours*

1 envelope unflavored gelatin
¼ cup water
1 cup milk
3 large egg yolks
⅓ cup granulated sugar
5 envelopes premelted
   unsweetened chocolate
1 cup heavy cream
GARNISH
Chocolate Whipped Cream
   (see page 125)
Chocolate Curls (see page 122) for
   garnish
Sliced fresh fruit for garnish

1 Lightly grease a 1-quart mold or serving dish.

2 In a cup, sprinkle the gelatin over the water. Let stand for 10 minutes to soften.

3 In a medium saucepan, over medium-low heat, combine the milk, egg yolks, and sugar, and cook, stirring constantly, for about 7 minutes, or until thickened. Remove from the heat.

4 Using an electric mixer on medium speed, beat the gelatin into the custard mixture and pour into a large bowl. On low speed, gradually beat in the chocolate. Beat for about 7 to 10 minutes, or until very thick. Cool to room temperature. Cover and chill for 10 to 15 minutes. Do not allow to set completely.

5 In a medium bowl, using an electric mixer on high speed, whip the cream until soft peaks form. Gently fold into the chilled chocolate mixture. Pour the mixture into the prepared mold, cover, and chill for at least 4 hours.

6 To unmold, dip the bowl into a large bowl of warm water for 15 to 20 seconds. Dry the bottom of the bowl. Run a knife around the inside edge and invert onto a serving plate. If the pudding does not slip out easily, dip the bowl in the warm water again. Smooth the top and sides with a spatula and chill for at least 1 hour, or until ready to serve. Serve with chocolate whipped cream and garnish with chocolate curls and thin slices of fresh fruit.

Baked chocolate
mousse cake

Yield: *16 servings*
baking time: *50 minutes*
chill time: *2 hours*

15 ounces semi-sweet chocolate,
    grated or finely chopped
2 cups butter or margarine
7 large eggs, separated, plus 7 large
    egg yolks
¾ cup granulated sugar
2 teaspoons chocolate or
    vanilla extract
½ cup fresh raspberries
1 sprig fresh mint for garnish

1 Position a rack in the center of
the oven and preheat the oven to
300 degrees. Lightly grease a 9-inch
springform pan.

2 In the top of a double boiler over
simmering water, melt the chocolate and butter, stirring until
smooth. Remove from the heat.

3 In a large bowl placed over a
pan of hot water, whisk the egg
yolks and the sugar until blended.
Remove bowl from the pan of
water. Using an electric mixer on
medium speed, beat until thick
and light-colored. Pouring it in a
thin stream, beat in the chocolate
mixture and chocolate extract on
low speed.

4 In a medium bowl, using an
electric mixer on high speed, beat
the egg whites until stiff peaks
form. Gently fold the beaten
whites into the chocolate mixture.

5 Pour two-thirds of the batter into
the prepared pan. Cover the
remaining batter in the bowl.

6 Bake for 45 to 50 minutes, or
until a cake tester inserted into the
center comes out clean. Cool in the
pan on a wire rack. The center will
sink and the cake will crack.

7 Using a piece of waxed paper or
a very flat plate, press down on the
raised portion of the cake to make
it level with the sunken portion.
Pour the reserved batter over the
top. Cover the pan and chill for at
least 2 hours. Remove from refrigerator 1 hour before serving.

8 To serve, remove from the pan
and place the cake on a serving
plate. Cut the raspberries in half
and arrange on top of the cake.
The mint may be used in one piece
or the leaves may be removed and
placed around the raspberries.

Baking notes: **Due to the raw eggs
used in this recipe, it should be kept
refrigerated at all times, and for no
longer than 3 days.**

Baked chocolate pudding

YIELD: *6 to 8 servings*
BAKING TIME: *45 minutes*

6 ounces unsweetened chocolate,
  grated or finely chopped
6 large eggs, separated
½ cup butter or margarine,
  at room temperature
1 cup powdered sugar
1 teaspoon crème de cacao
5 tablespoons arrowroot or
  cornstarch
1 cup milk
1 cup heavy cream
Kahlúa Cocoa Sauce (see page 127)
  for serving

1 Position a rack in the center of the oven and preheat the oven to 350 degrees. Lightly grease a 1½-quart casserole dish.

2 Melt the chocolate. Remove from the heat.

3 In a large bowl, using an electric mixer on high speed, beat the egg whites until stiff but not dry.

4 In another large bowl, using an electric mixer on medium speed, beat the butter and powdered sugar until fluffy. Beat in the crème de cacao. Beat in the egg yolks, one at a time, beating well after each addition. Pouring it in a steady stream, beat in the melted chocolate on low speed. Combine the arrowroot and milk and stir into the chocolate mixture. Stir in the cream. Fold in the egg whites. Pour the mixture into the prepared casserole dish.

5 Bake for 40 to 45 minutes, or until a cake tester inserted into the center comes out clean. Cool slightly and serve with Kahlúa sauce.

Barriga de freira

YIELD: *8 to 10 servings*

1½ cups granulated sugar
½ cup water
¾ cup finely ground almonds
½ cup dried bread crumbs
3 large eggs
4 ounces unsweetened chocolate,
  grated or finely chopped
1 cup milk or heavy cream

1 In a medium saucepan, over low heat, combine 1 cup of the sugar and the water. Cook, stirring occasionally, until the sugar is dissolved. Using a pastry brush dipped in cold water, wash down the sugar crystals on the side of the pan. Raise the heat to medium and bring to a boil. Cook, without stirring, for 2 minutes. Remove from the heat and immediately stir in the almonds and bread crumbs. Cover and let stand for 3 minutes.

2 In a medium bowl, using an electric mixer on medium speed, beat the eggs until thick and light-colored.

3 Stir the beaten eggs into the sugar mixture. Cook over medium heat, stirring constantly, until thickened. Do not allow the mixture to boil. Remove from the heat and transfer to serving bowl.

4 In the top of a double boiler over simmering water, melt the chocolate, stirring constantly until smooth. Stir in the milk and the remaining ½ cup sugar. Cook, stirring constantly, until smooth. Stir into the egg mixture. Cool to room temperature before serving.

BITTER-SWEET CHOCOLATE MOUSSE

YIELD: *4 to 6 servings*
CHILL TIME: *4 hours*

3 large eggs, separated
¾ cup plus 1 tablespoon powdered
  sugar
5 ounces unsweetened chocolate,
  grated or finely chopped
¼ cup butter or margarine, at room
  temperature
3 tablespoons raspberry liqueur
1 teaspoon chocolate or
  vanilla extract
3 tablespoons strong brewed coffee
½ cup heavy cream

1 In a small bowl, using an electric
mixer on high speed, beat the egg
whites until stiff peaks form. Fold
in 1 tablespoon of the powdered
sugar.

2 Melt the chocolate. Remove from
the heat and stir in the butter.

3 In the top of a double boiler,
over simmering water blend the
egg yolks, the remaining ¾ cup
powdered sugar, the raspberry
liqueur, and chocolate extract.
Using a wire whisk, beat well until
the mixture is thick. Place over
simmering water and stir constantly for about 5 minutes, or until the
mixture is foamy. Remove from the
heat. Blend the chocolate mixture
into the egg yolk mixture. Beat in
the coffee and cool for 5 minutes.
Fold in the egg whites into the
mixture, stirring until completely
blended.

4 In a small bowl, using an electric
mixer on high speed, whip the
cream until soft peaks form. Fold
the whipped cream into the chocolate mixture. Spoon the mixture
into four to six chilled custard cups
or a chilled serving bowl. Chill for
4 hours, or until ready to serve.

BAKING NOTES: Due to the raw eggs
in this recipe, it should be kept
refrigerated at all times, and for no
longer than 1 week.

BLACK FOREST PARFAITS

YIELD: *4 to 6 servings*
CHILL TIME: *30 minutes*

3 ounces cream cheese, at room
  temperature
2 cups minus 2 tablespoons milk
1 package (3.4 ounces) Jell-O Brand
  chocolate instant pudding mix
1½ tablespoons Kümmel liqueur or
  Aquavit
½ cup chocolate wafer cookie crumbs
1 can (21 ounces) cherry pie filling
Whipped cream for garnish
Ground hazelnuts for garnish

1 In a small bowl, using an electric
mixer on medium speed, beat the
cream cheese and ½ cup of the milk
until smooth. Beat in the pudding
mix and the remaining milk. Add
the liqueur and beat for 2 minutes.

2 Spoon half of the mixture evenly
into four to six chilled parfait
glasses. Sprinkle with chocolate
wafer crumbs and cover with the
pie filling. Top with the remaining
pudding and chill for 30 minutes,
or until ready to serve. Garnish
with whipped cream and sprinkle
with ground hazelnuts.

BLENDER CHOCOLATE MOUSSE

YIELD: *4 servings*
CHILL TIME: *8 hours*

1 large egg
1 envelope unflavored gelatin
1 tablespoon cornstarch or arrowroot
1 tablespoon cold water
1 cup boiling water
2 tablespoons mocha-flavored instant coffee powder
½ cup ricotta cheese
½ cup skim milk, chilled
2 tablespoons Dutch processed cocoa powder
½ cup granulated sugar
⅛ teaspoon salt

1 In the container of a blender, combine the egg, gelatin, cornstarch, and cold water. Blend for 20 seconds. Add the boiling water and blend for 30 seconds. Add the coffee powder, ricotta cheese, skim milk, cocoa powder, sugar, and salt, and blend for about a minute, or until smooth.

2 Pour into four chilled custard cups and chill overnight or until set.

BAKING NOTES: Due to the raw egg in this recipe, it should be kept refrigerated at all times, and for no longer than 3 days.

CHOCOLATE APPLE PUDDING

YIELD: *12 to 16 servings*
BAKING TIME: *50 minutes*

2 ounce semi-sweet chocolate, grated or finely chopped
2 cups granulated sugar
1 cup hot water
½ cup crème de cacao
2¼ cups all-purpose flour
2 teaspoons baking powder
1 teaspoon baking soda
1½ teaspoons ground allspice
½ cup butter or margarine, at room temperature
4 cups chopped apples
Chocolate Whipped Cream (see page 125) for serving

1 Position a rack in the center of the oven and preheat the oven to 350 degrees. Lightly grease a 2½-quart casserole dish.

2 In the top of a double boiler over simmering water, melt the chocolate, stirring until smooth. Stir in 1 cup of the sugar, blending until dissolved. Remove from the heat and stir in the hot water and crème de cacao.

3 In a large bowl, combine the remaining 1 cup sugar, the flour, baking powder, baking soda, and allspice. Using a pastry blender or two knives scissor fashion, cut in the butter to make a crumbly mixture. Fold in the apples.

4 To assemble, spread one-third of the apple mixture onto the bottom of the prepared casserole. Pour one-third of the chocolate mixture over the top. Repeat with the remaining apple and chocolate mixtures, ending with the chocolate mixture. Carefully swirl a spoon through the layers until the apple mixture is just moistened.

5 Bake for 45 to 50 minutes, or until thickened.

6 Make the chocolate whipped cream. Serve the pudding warm from the oven topped with the chocolate whipped cream.

BAKING NOTES: Coffee liqueur can be substituted for the crème de cacao.

CHOCOLATE BROWN BETTY

YIELD: *6 to 8 servings*
BAKING TIME: *1 hour*

⅓ cup butter or margarine, melted
2 cups whole-wheat bread crumbs
¼ teaspoon ground cinnamon
¼ teaspoon ground nutmeg
½ cup granulated sugar
2 cups cored, peeled, and diced
    apples
½ cup Chocolate Syrup I
    (see page 125)
1 tablespoon water
Juice of one lemon
Grated zest of one lemon
Chocolate Whipped Cream
    (see page 125) for serving

1 Position a rack in the center of the oven and preheat the oven to 350 degrees. Lightly grease a 9-inch square pan.

2 In a medium bowl, using an electric mixer on low speed, drizzle the melted butter over the bread crumbs while beating. Stir in the spices and sugar. Press one-third of the crumb mixture onto the bottom of the prepared pan. Spread half of the diced apples evenly over the top of the crumbs. Sprinkle half of the remaining crumbs over the apples. Spread the remaining apples over the crumbs and top with the remaining crumbs.

3 Combine the chocolate syrup, water, lemon juice, and zest. Spoon evenly over the top of the mixture in the pan, making sure all portions have been covered.

4 Cover with aluminum foil and bake for 30 minutes. Remove the foil and bake for an additional 30 minutes, or until crust forms on top. Cool in the pan for 15 minutes. Serve with the chocolate whipped cream on the side.

BAKING NOTES: Almost any fruit or combination of fruits can be used in place of the apples.

CHOCOLATE CHOCOLATE MOUSSE

YIELD: *8 to 10 servings*
FREEZING TIME: *4 hours*

3 ounces unsweetened chocolate,
    grated or finely chopped
⅓ cup crème de cacao
¾ cup granulated sugar
Pinch of salt
3 large egg yolks
2 cups heavy cream
1 teaspoon chocolate or
    vanilla extract
Fresh mint sprigs for garnish
Sliced orange or peeled and sliced
    kiwifruit for garnish

1 In the top of a double boiler over simmering water, melt the chocolate, stirring until smooth. Stir in the crème de cacao. Add the sugar and salt and continue to cook, stirring constantly, until the sugar is dissolved and the mixture is smooth. Remove from the heat.

2 In a large bowl, using an electric mixer on medium speed, beat the egg yolks until thick and light-colored. Pouring it in a thin stream, beat in the chocolate mixture until well blended. Set aside to cool to room temperature.

3 In a large bowl, using an electric mixer on high speed, whip the cream and chocolate extract until soft peaks form. Fold into the chocolate mixture and pour into a serving bowl. Cover and freeze for 3 to 4 hours or until ready to serve. Remove from the freezer 30 minutes before serving. Garnish with fresh mint and slices of oranges or kiwifruits.

BAKING NOTES: Due to the raw egg in this recipe, it should be kept refrigerated at all times, and for no longer than 3 days.

Chocolate
COFFEE CHARLOTTE

Yield: *6 to 8 servings*
chill time: *6½ hours*

36 ladyfingers, split
6 ounces semi-sweet chocolate, grated or finely chopped
2 cups milk
2 teaspoons unflavored gelatin
¼ cup water
5 large egg yolks
¼ cup granulated sugar
1 teaspoon chocolate or vanilla extract
3 tablespoon coffee liqueur
½ cup heavy cream
Cocoa Sugar (see page 125) for dusting
Chocolate Whipped Cream (see page 125) for garnish
Fresh mint leaves for garnish

1 Line the bottom and sides of a straight-sided 1½- to 2-quart mold with waxed or parchment paper. Lightly butter the paper. (Do not use oil or a non-stick spray.)

2 Line the bottom and sides of the mold with ladyfingers, trimming them to fit as needed. The ladyfingers should be fitted as tightly as possible. The tips of the ladyfingers may extend above the mold. Trim if desired or leave the rounded ends. Chill until ready to fill.

3 Melt the chocolate. Remove from the heat.

4 In a large saucepan, over medium-low heat, heat the milk until bubbles start to form around the sides of the pan. Remove from the heat.

5 In a small saucepan, sprinkle the gelatin over the water and let stand for 1 minute to soften. Over low heat, stir until the gelatin is completely dissolved. Remove from the heat.

6 In a large bowl, using an electric mixer on medium speed, beat the egg yolks until thick and light-colored. Beat in the sugar. Beating constantly, beat in half of the hot milk. Pour the mixture back into the remaining milk in the saucepan and beat on high speed for 1 to 2 minutes. Return to the heat and cook, stirring constantly, until the mixture thickens enough to coat the back of a spoon. (Do not allow the mixture to boil.) Strain into a large bowl. Beat in the gelatin and add the chocolate extract. Pouring it in a thin stream, beat in the melted chocolate. Stir in the coffee liqueur. Cover and chill for 30 minutes.

7 In a medium bowl, using an electric mixer on high speed, beat the cream until soft peaks form. Fold the whipped cream into the chilled chocolate custard mixture. Immediately pour into the prepared mold. Cover and chill for 4 to 6 hours.

8 When ready to serve, remove from the mold and place on a serving plate. Remove the waxed paper and sift a light coating of cocoa sugar over the top. Fill a pastry bag filled with a large star tip with the chocolate whipped cream and pipe rosettes around the base of the charlotte. Place a mint leaf on each rosette.

CHOCOLATE CREAM PUDDING

YIELD: *6 to 8 servings*
CHILL TIME: *4 hours*

1⅓ cups chocolate graham cracker crumbs
½ cup plus 2 tablespoons packed light-brown sugar
3 ounces semi-sweet chocolate, grated or finely chopped
1 tablespoon Dutch processed cocoa powder
1 teaspoon instant espresso powder
2 cups heavy cream
Chocolate Whipped Cream (see page 125) for garnish
Chocolate Curls (see page 122) for garnish

1 In a medium bowl, combine the graham cracker crumbs, brown sugar, grated chocolate, cocoa powder, and espresso powder.

2 In a large bowl, using an electric mixer on high speed, whip the cream until slightly thickened.

3 To assemble, pour one-fourth of the cream into a serving bowl. Top with one-third of the crumb mixture. Repeat with the remaining cream and crumb mixture. Cover and chill for 4 hours.

4 When ready to serve, serve with chocolate whipped cream and chocolate curls on the side.

CHOCOLATE CUSTARD II

YIELD: *8 servings*
BAKING TIME: *90 minutes*
CHILL TIME: *80 minutes*

3 ounces unsweetened chocolate, grated or finely chopped
3 ounces semi-sweet chocolate, grated or finely chopped
2 tablespoons butter or margarine
6 large eggs
½ cup granulated sugar
3⅓ cups milk
2 teaspoons chocolate or vanilla extract

1 Position a rack in the center of the oven and preheat the oven to 350 degrees.

2 Combine the chocolates and butter in a 1½-quart casserole dish and heat in the oven for 3 to 5 minutes. Remove from the oven and stir until blended. Chill for 20 minutes, or until the mixture is just starting to set. Using a spatula, spread evenly over the bottom and sides of the casserole dish. Chill for 30 minutes.

3 In a large bowl, using an electric mixer on medium speed, beat the eggs until thick and light-colored. Add the sugar, milk, and chocolate extract and beat until the sugar is completely dissolved. Pour the mixture into the chilled casserole. Place the casserole dish in a roasting pan on the oven rack. Pour boiling water into the pan until it comes halfway up the sides of the casserole dish.

4 Bake for 80 to 90 minutes, or until a cake tester inserted into the center comes out clean. Remove from the hot water and chill for 30 minutes, or until ready to serve.

Chocolate
Liqueur Cream

Yield: *8 to 10 servings*
chill time: *2 hours*

4 ounces semi-sweet chocolate,
   grated or finely chopped
4 large eggs, separated
½ cup granulated sugar
½ cup heavy cream
4 tablespoons crème de cacao
Whipped cream for garnish

1 In the top of a double boiler over simmering water, melt the chocolate, stirring until smooth. Remove from the heat.

2 In a large bowl, using an electric mixer on medium speed, beat the egg yolks until thick and light-colored. Beat in ¼ cup of the sugar. Beat in the melted chocolate, blending until no streaks appear. Beat in the cream. Return the mixture to the double boiler and cook over low heat until the mixture has thickened slightly. Remove from the heat.

3 In a medium bowl, using an electric mixer on high speed, beat the egg whites until stiff but not dry. Beat in the remaining ¼ cup sugar. Fold into the chocolate mixture and fold in the crème de cacao. Cover and chill for at least 2 hours.

4 To serve, spoon into eight to ten dessert cups and garnish with whipped cream.

Chocolate
MOCHA MOUSSE

Yield: *8 to 10 servings*
CHILL TIME: *24 hours*

Chocolate Cookie Crumb Crust
  (see page 122)
⅓ cup amaretto
1 tablespoon unflavored gelatin
4 large egg yolks
½ cup granulated sugar
¾ cup coffee liqueur
8 ounces unsweetened chocolate,
  grated or finely chopped
4 ounces semi-sweet chocolate,
  grated or finely chopped
1 tablespoon instant espresso
  powder
¼ cup butter or margarine, at room
  temperature
1 cup heavy cream
Fresh mint sprigs for garnish
Chocolate Leaves (see page 128)
  for garnish

1 Make the crust. Press half of the
mixture onto the bottom of an 8 or
9-inch springform pan. Cover the
remaining crust mixture and set
aside at room temperature.

2 In a cup, combine the amaretto
and gelatin. Let stand 1 minute to
soften.

3 In the top of a double boiler,
using a wire whisk, beat the egg
yolks and sugar until blended. Stir
in the coffee liqueur. Set over simmering water and beat until the
mixture starts to thicken. Remove
from the heat and stir in the softened gelatin. Set the top of the
double boiler in a large bowl of ice
and water and beat for about 5
minutes, or until the mixture is
room temperature. Remove from
the bowl of ice water.

4 In the top of a double boiler over
simmering water, melt the chocolates, stirring until smooth. Add
the espresso powder and stir until
dissolved and smooth. Transfer to

a large bowl. Using an electric
mixer on medium speed, beat in
the butter, a little at a time, blending thoroughly after each addition.
Add the egg yolk mixture and beat
until thickened and cooled to room
temperature. Set the bowl in the
bowl of ice and water and continue
beating until the mixture is completely cool.

5 In a medium bowl, using an
electric mixer on high speed, whip
the cream until soft peaks form.
Fold the whipped cream into the
cooled chocolate mixture. Pour
into the prepared pan and spread
evenly. Cover and chill for 24
hours.

6 To serve, remove from the springform pan and place the mousse on
a serving plate. Sprinkle the reserved
crust mixture over the top and press
it against the sides of the mousse.
Garnish with chocolate leaves and
mint sprigs.

Chocolate
MOCHA SOUFFLÉ

YIELD: *8 to 10 servings*
BAKING TIME: *40 minutes*

3 ounces unsweetened chocolate,
grated or finely chopped
4 large eggs, separated, plus 1 large
egg white
3 tablespoons butter
2 tablespoons all-purpose flour
1 cup milk
½ cup granulated sugar
1 tablespoon coffee liqueur
1 teaspoon crème de cacao
Pinch of salt
Whipped cream for serving

1 Position a rack in the center of
the oven and preheat the oven to
350 degrees. Lightly grease and
dust with sugar a 1½-quart soufflé
dish. Wrap a strip of aluminum foil
or parchment paper around the top
of the dish so that it extends 2
inches above the rim and tie
securely with string.

2 Melt the chocolate. Remove from
the heat.

3 In a small bowl, using an electric
mixer on medium speed, beat the
egg yolks until thick and light-colored.

4 In a medium bowl, using an electric mixer on high speed, beat the
egg whites until stiff but not dry.

5 In a large saucepan, over medium heat, melt the butter. Stir in the
flour to make a roux. Stir in the
milk. Cook, stirring constantly,

until the mixture is thickened and
smooth. Add the sugar and melted
chocolate. Mix in the beaten egg
yolks and cook, stirring constantly,
for 2 to 3 minutes. Remove from
the heat and stir in the liqueurs
and salt. Fold in the beaten egg
whites. Do not overmix. Pour the
mixture into the prepared dish.
Place soufflé dish in a roasting pan
on the oven rack. Pour boiling
water into the pan until it come
halfway up the sides of the soufflé
dish.

6 Bake for 35 to 40 minutes, or
until a cake tester inserted into the
center comes out clean.

**BAKING NOTES: For a decorative gar-
nish, just before serving, place an
overlapping ring of peeled, thinly
sliced kiwi fruit, and/or thinly
sliced strawberries, on the top of
the soufflé.**

CHOCOLATE MOUSSE À L'ORANGE

YIELD: *8 to 10 servings*
CHILL TIME: *10 hours*

8 ounces semi-sweet chocolate,
  grated or finely chopped
3 tablespoons marshmallow creme
2 tablespoons thawed frozen orange
  juice concentrate
4 large eggs, separated
½ teaspoon cream of tartar
Whipped cream for garnish
Grated orange zest for garnish

1 In the top of a double boiler over
simmering water, melt the chocolate, stirring constantly until
smooth. Add the marshmallow
creme and orange juice concentrate, stirring until blended and
smooth. Remove from the heat.

2 In a large bowl, using an electric
mixer on high speed, beat the egg
whites until foamy. Add the cream
of tartar and continue beating until
stiff peaks form.

3 In a small bowl, using an electric
mixer on high speed, beat the egg
yolks until thick and light-colored.
Beat in the chocolate mixture. Gently
fold into the egg whites, blending
thoroughly. Spoon the mixture into
eight to ten custard cups or
ramekins and chill for 8 to 10 hours
before serving. Just before serving
top with whipped cream and
sprinkle with grated orange zest.

BAKING NOTES: The mousse can also
be chilled in a 9 or 10-inch serving
bowl. Due to the raw eggs in this
recipe, it should be kept refrigerated
at all times, and for no longer than 3
days.

CHOCOLATE RASPBERRY SOUFFLÉ

YIELD: *6 servings*
CHILL TIME: *30 minutes*

1 cup fresh raspberries
2 tablespoons granulated sugar
1 envelope unflavored gelatin
¼ cup boiling water
2 large egg whites
1 jar (7 ounces) marshmallow creme
1 cup heavy cream
2 ounces semi-sweet chocolate,
  grated or finely chopped
½ cup whole fresh raspberries for
  garnish
Chocolate Curls (see page 122) for
  garnish

1 Wrap a strip of aluminum foil or
parchment paper around the top of
a 3-cup soufflé dish so that it extends
2 inches above the rim and tie
securely with string.

2 In a small bowl, mash the raspberries. Strain through a sieve into
another bowl. Stir in the sugar and
let stand for at least 10 minutes.

3 In a cup, sprinkle the gelatin
over boiling water and stir until
dissolved. Stir into the raspberries
and chill until thickened but not
set.

4 In a medium bowl, using an
electric mixer on high speed, beat
the egg whites until soft peaks form.
Gradually add the marshmallow
creme, a little at a time, beating until
stiff peaks form. Fold the raspberry
mixture into the egg whites.

5 In a large bowl, using an electric
mixer on high speed, beat the
cream until soft peaks form. Fold
into the raspberry mixture. Fold in
the grated chocolate. Pour the mixture into the prepared soufflé dish
and chill 30 minutes, or until firm.

6 To serve, remove soufflé from
the dish. Remove the foil strip.
Transfer onto a serving plate and
garnish with fresh raspberries and
chocolate curls.

CHOCOLATE RICE PUDDING

YIELD: *4 to 6 servings*
CHILL TIME: *1 hour*

2 cups milk
⅓ cup long-grain rice, uncooked
3 tablespoons Dutch processed cocoa
  powder
¼ cup granulated sugar
½ teaspoon chocolate or
  vanilla extract
Fresh mint sprigs or peeled and
  sliced kiwifruit for garnish
Chocolate Sauce III (see page 124) for
  serving

1 Rinse four to six 4-ounce custard
cups or pudding glasses in cold
water. Do not try.

2 In the top of a double boiler over
simmering water, combine the
milk, rice, and cocoa powder.
Cover and cook, stirring occasionally, for 15 to 20 minutes, or until
the mixture is quite thick. Add the
sugar and stir until dissolved.
Remove from the heat and stir in
the chocolate extract. Immediately
pour the mixture into the prepared
custard cups. Chill for 1 hour, or
until set.

3 Invert the set puddings onto
individual dessert plates. Garnish
with mint sprigs or thinly sliced
kiwifruit. Serve with chocolate
sauce on the side.

CHOCOLATE RUM MOUSSE

YIELD: *6 to 8 servings*
CHILL TIME: *3 to 5 hours*

½ cup milk
½ cup heavy cream
2 large eggs, at room temperature
2 tablespoons butter or margarine, at
  room temperature
6 ounces semi-sweet chocolate,
  grated or finely chopped
1 teaspoon rum or rum extract
Chocolate Whipped Cream
  (see page 125)
Chocolate Curls for garnish
  (see page 122)

1 Lightly butter six pudding glasses
or custard cups.

2 In a medium saucepan, over low
heat, warm the milk and cream
until bubbles start to form around
the sides of the pan.

3 In the container of a blender,
combine the eggs, butter, chocolate, and rum. Blend on medium
speed until smooth. Add the warm
milk and blend for a few seconds
until slightly thickened.

4 Pour the mixture into the prepared pudding glasses and chill for
3 to 5 hours, or until set.

5 When ready to serve, place a dab
of chocolate whipped cream on the
top of each and sprinkle with
chocolate curls.

COFFEE RAISIN FROZEN CHOCOLATE FUDGE

YIELD: *8 to 10 servings*
FREEZING TIME: *1 hour*

½ cup raisins
⅓ cup coffee liqueur
4 ounces semi-sweet chocolate, grated or finely chopped
3 ounces unsweetened chocolate, grated or finely chopped
1 ounce white chocolate or almond bark, grated or finely chopped
½ cup butter or margarine, at room temperature
¼ cup Dutch processed cocoa powder
5 tablespoons boiling water
4 large eggs, separated
⅓ cup granulated sugar
Pinch of salt
Chocolate Sauce V (see page 124) for serving

1 Combine the raisins and liqueur in an airtight container and cover. Soak the raisins for at least 24 hours.

2 In the top of a double boiler over simmering water, melt the chocolates, stirring until smooth. Remove from the heat.

3 In a cup, blend the cocoa powder and boiling water until smooth. Stir into the melted chocolate.

4 In a large bowl, using an electric mixer on medium speed, beat the egg yolks and butter until thick and light-colored. Beat in the sugar.

5 Beat the chocolate mixture into the egg yolks until smooth. Fold in the raisins and liqueur. Freeze for 1 hour, or until thickened. Do not allow to set.

6 In a large bowl, using an electric mixer on high speed, beat the egg whites and salt until stiff but not dry. Fold into the chilled chocolate mixture. Cover and freeze until firm. Spoon the fudge into a serving bowl and serve with chocolate sauce on the side.

EASY CHOCOLATE MOUSSE

YIELD: *8 to 10 servings*
CHILL TIME: *2 hours*

12 ounces semi-sweet chocolate, grated or finely chopped
5 large eggs, separated
2 cups heavy cream

1 Melt the chocolate. Remove from the heat and cool to room temperature.

2 In a large bowl, using an electric mixer on high speed, beat the egg whites until stiff but not dry.

3 In a medium bowl, using an electric mixer on medium speed, beat the egg yolks until thick and light-colored.

4 In another medium bowl, using an electric mixer on high speed, whip the cream until soft peaks form.

5 Beat the chocolate into the egg yolks until smooth and yellow streaks no longer appear. Fold in one-third of the egg whites into the chocolate mixture. Fold the chocolate mixture back into the remaining egg whites until streaks no longer appear. Fold in the whipped cream. Spoon the mousse into a large glass serving bowl. Cover and chill for 1 to 2 hours, or until ready to serve.

BAKING NOTES: Due to the raw eggs in this recipe, it should be kept refrigerated at all times, and for no longer than 3 days.

ENGLISH CHOCOLATE PUDDING

YIELD: *6 servings*
STEAMING TIME: *90 minutes*

2 ounces unsweetened chocolate, grated or finely chopped
½ cup milk
2 tablespoons butter, or margarine at room temperature
½ cup granulated sugar
2 large eggs, separated
½ cup bread or cake crumbs
1½ teaspoons chocolate or vanilla extract
Chocolate Custard Sauce (see page 122) for serving

1 Generously grease six ½-cup heatproof molds or one 3-cup mold.

2 In the top of a double boiler over simmering water, melt the chocolate with the milk, stirring until smooth. Remove from the heat.

3 In a medium bowl, using an electric mixer on medium speed, beat the butter and sugar until light and fluffy. Beat in the egg yolks. Beat in the crumbs and chocolate extract. Stir in the chocolate mixture.

4 In a small bowl, using an electric mixer on high speed, beat the egg whites until stiff but not dry. Fold into the chocolate mixture. Divide the mixture evenly between the prepared molds. Cover tightly with aluminum foil. Prick the foil several times.

5 Place in a steamer or pot with enough water to cover the bottom by 2 inches and cover. Steam over medium-low heat for 90 minutes. Cool completely on wire racks without removing the foil covers. Serve with chocolate custard sauce on the side.

BAKING NOTES: Traditionally, the puddings are covered with a piece of cloth and it is tied in place with string. Today, they can be covered with a piece of aluminum foil. Tightly fit the foil over the top of the mold and down the sides. Prick the top of the foil several times with a needle.

FROZEN NESSELRODE CHOCOLATE PUDDING

YIELD: *6 to 8 servings*
FREEZING TIME: *2 hours*

3 large egg yolks
1½ cups half-and-half
1 can (10 ounces) crushed pineapple in juice
¾ cup granulated sugar
1 envelope unflavored gelatin
¼ teaspoon salt
1 cup heavy cream
½ cup golden raisins
2 tablespoons diced maraschino cherries
3 ounces semi-sweet chocolate, grated or finely chopped

1 In a medium saucepan, using an electric mixer on medium speed, beat the egg yolks until thick and light-colored. Add the half-and-half, pineapple with its juice, sugar, gelatin, and salt and cook over medium-low heat, stirring constantly, for about 5 to 7 minutes, or until slightly thickened. Pour into a shallow pan, cover, and freeze for 2 hours.

2 In a medium bowl, using an electric mixer on high speed, beat the cream until stiff peaks form.

3 Transfer the partially frozen custard to a medium bowl. Using an electric mixer on high speed, beat until smooth. Fold in the whipped cream, raisins, cherries, and grated chocolate. Pour into a 2-quart mold or back into the shallow dish. Cover and freeze until firm. To serve, dip the bottom of the mold into a bowl of warm water for a few seconds. Dry the bottom of the mold and invert onto a serving plate. Or scoop out of the dish and serve in dessert cups.

GRAND MARNIER MOUSSE

YIELD: *6 to 8 servings*
CHILL TIME: *2 hours*

1 cup heavy cream
¼ cup granulated sugar
½ cup fresh orange juice, strained
8 ounces semi-sweet chocolate,
  grated or finely chopped
3 large egg yolks
¼ cup Grand Marnier

1 In a medium bowl, using an electric mixer on high speed, whip the cream until soft peaks form.

2 In the top of a double boiler over simmering water, warm the sugar and orange juice. Add the chocolate and stir constantly until it is melted and smooth. Remove from the heat.

3 In a medium bowl, using an electric mixer on medium speed, beat the egg yolks until thick and light-colored. Pouring it in a thin stream, beat in the chocolate mixture on low speed. Fold in the whipped cream and Grand Marnier. Pour into a serving bowl and chill for at least 2 hours, or until ready to serve.

BAKING NOTES: Due to the raw eggs in this recipe, it should be kept refrigerated at all times, and for no longer than 3 days.

Mocha chocolate soufflés

YIELD: *6 servings*
BAKING TIME: *20 minutes*

CHOCOLATE SOUFFLÉS
¼ cup Cocoa Sugar (see page 125)
4 ounces unsweetened chocolate, grated or finely chopped
1 cup milk
½ cup granulated sugar
3 large eggs, separated, plus 9 large egg whites
2 tablespoons all-purpose flour
1 teaspoon Swiss chocolate almond liqueur

COFFEE CUSTARD SAUCE
1½ cups heavy cream
1½ tablespoons mocha-flavored instant coffee powder
6 large egg yolks
¼ cup granulated sugar

1 Position a rack in the center of the oven and preheat the oven to 375 degrees. Lightly grease six 1-cup ramekins. Sprinkle generously with the cocoa sugar.

2 To make the soufflés, melt the chocolate. Remove from the heat.

3 In a saucepan, over medium heat, combine the milk and ¼ cup of the sugar and stir constantly until the mixture boils. Remove from the heat.

4 In a medium bowl, using an electric mixer on medium speed, beat the egg yolks until thick and light-colored. Beat in the remaining ¼ cup sugar. Add the flour and blend just until mixed. Gradually mix in the hot milk and beat for 1 minute. Pour the mixture back into the saucepan. Bring to a boil, stirring constantly, and cook until thick and smooth. Remove from the heat. Strain the mixture through a sieve into a large bowl. Stir in the liqueur and melted chocolate.

5 In a large bowl, using an electric mixer on high speed, beat the egg whites until soft peaks form. One-third at a time, fold the egg whites into the custard mixture. Spoon into the prepared ramekins. Set the cups in a roasting pan and place on the oven rack. Pour boiling water into the roasting pan until it comes halfway up the sides of the ramekins.

6 Bake for 15 to 20 minutes, or until the soufflés puff up and a cake tester inserted into the center comes out clean. Remove from the hot water.

7 To make the sauce, in a medium saucepan, over medium heat, heat the cream until bubbles start to form around the sides of the pan. Remove from the heat. Stir in the coffee powder until it is dissolved.

8 In a medium bowl, using an electric mixer on medium speed, beat the egg yolks until thick and light-colored. Beat in the sugar. Pouring it in a thin stream, beat in the hot cream. Pour the mixture back into the saucepan and cook over low heat, stirring constantly, until thick. Do not allow to boil. Remove from the heat and immediately strain through a sieve into a small bowl. Cover with plastic wrap and keep warm until ready to use.

9 While still warm, open the top of each soufflé and spoon ¾ of a teaspoonful of sauce into each pudding. Serve the remaining sauce on the side.

Mocha pudding cake

YIELD: *10 to 12 servings*
CHILL TIME: *6 hours*

Pots au chocolat I

YIELD: 6 TO 8 SERVINGS
CHILL TIME: *8 hours*

18 ladyfingers, split
1 envelope unflavored gelatin
2 tablespoons coffee liqueur
1 cup semi-sweet chocolate chips
8 ounces cream cheese, at room temperature
½ cup packed light brown sugar
1 teaspoon instant espresso powder
½ cup heavy cream
1½ teaspoons chocolate or vanilla extract
1½ cups Chocolate Whipped Cream (see page 125) for garnish
Chocolate Curls (see page 122) for garnish

1 To make the cake, line the bottom and sides of a 9-inch springform pan with the ladyfingers, trimming them to fit as needed.

2 In a cup, sprinkle the gelatin over the liqueur. Let stand for 1 minute to soften. Place the cup in a pan of hot water and stir until the gelatin is dissolved.

3 Melt the chocolate chips. Remove from the heat and transfer to a large bowl. Using an electric mixer on medium speed, beat in the cream cheese, ¼ cup of the brown sugar, and the espresso powder until blended and smooth. Beat in the gelatin mixture.

4 In a medium bowl, using an electric mixer on high speed, beat the cream until soft peaks form. Add the remaining ¼ cup of the brown sugar and the chocolate extract and beat until stiff peaks form. Fold the cream into the chocolate mixture. Pour into the prepared pan and spread evenly. Cover and chill for 5 to 6 hours or overnight, or until set.

5 Make the chocolate whipped cream and the chocolate curls.

6 To serve, carefully remove the side of the springform pan and place the cake on a serving plate. Drop large dabs of the topping over the cake. Sprinkle with chocolate curls.

6 ounces semi-sweet chocolate, grated or finely chopped
¼ cup water
1 tablespoon butter or margarine
3 large eggs, separated
¼ cup cherry liqueur

1 In the top of a double boiler over simmering water, melt the chocolate with the water, stirring until smooth. Remove from the heat and beat in the butter. Using an electric mixer on medium speed, beat in the egg yolks and liqueur.

2 In a medium bowl, using an electric mixer on high speed, beat the egg whites until still but not dry. Fold into the chocolate mixture. Pour into six to eight chilled custard cups and chill overnight.

BAKING NOTES: Due to the raw eggs used in this recipe, it should be kept refrigerated at all times, and for no longer than 3 days.

Spiced chocolate bread pudding

Yield: *6 servings*
baking time: *70 minutes*

2½ cups heavy cream
2 ounces semi-sweet chocolate,
    grated or finely chopped
2 tablespoons butter or margarine
2 large eggs
3 tablespoons coffee liqueur
1 cup soft white bread, cut into ½-
    inch cubes
⅔ cup granulated sugar
½ teaspoon ground cinnamon
¼ teaspoon ground nutmeg
Pinch of salt
2 teaspoons chocolate extract
Chocolate Whipped Cream (see
    page 125) for serving

1 Position a rack in the center of
the oven and preheat the oven to
325 degrees. Lightly grease and
sugar a 1-quart soufflé dish or
casserole dish.

2 In a large saucepan, over medium heat, heat the cream until bubbles start to form around the sides
of the pan. Add the chocolate and
butter, stirring constantly, until
melted and smooth. Remove from
the heat and cool.

3 In a small bowl, using an electric
mixer on medium speed, beat the
eggs until thick and light-colored.
Beat in the liqueur.

4 In a large bowl, combine the
bread cubes, sugar, cinnamon,
nutmeg, and salt. Using a wooden
spoon, stir in the cream mixture.
Add the chocolate extract. Stir in
the egg mixture and pour into the
prepared baking dish and spread
evenly.

5 Bake for 65 to 70 minutes, or
until a cake tester inserted into the
center comes out clean.

6 Make the chocolate whipped
cream. Serve warm or cold with
chocolate whipped cream on the
side.

Upside-down chocolate pudding

Yield: *8 to 10 servings*
baking time: *35 minutes*

¼ cup butter or margarine
½ cup Dutch processed cocoa powder
1 cup all-purpose flour
¾ cup granulated sugar
3 tablespoons mocha-flavored
    instant coffee powder
1½ teaspoons baking powder
1 large egg
½ cup milk
1¼ cups boiling water
Chocolate Whipped Cream (see
    page 125) for garnish

1 Position a rack in the center of
the oven and preheat the oven to
350 degrees. Lightly grease a 1½-
quart casserole dish.

2 In a small saucepan, over low
heat, melt the butter, stirring until
smooth. Remove from the heat. Stir
in the cocoa until smooth.

3 Combine the flour, ½ cup of the
sugar, the coffee powder, and
baking powder.

4 In a small bowl, using an electric
mixer on high speed, beat the egg
until foamy. Beat in the milk. On
low speed, beat in the chocolate
mixture. Gradually blend in the dry
ingredients, a little at a time, blending
well after each addition. Pour into
the prepared casserole dish and
spread evenly.

5 Sprinkle ¼ cup sugar over the
batter in the casserole dish. Gently
pour the boiling water over the
cocoa mixture. Place the casserole
dish in a roasting pan on the oven
rack. Pour boiling water into the
pan until it comes halfway up the
sides of the casserole dish.

6 Bake for 30 to 35 minutes, or until
a cake tester inserted into the center
comes out clean. Cool for 15 to 30
minutes. Invert onto a serving plate.
To serve, spoon into individual serving dishes and top with chocolate
whipped cream.

ALMOND SCONES WITH CHOCOLATE SAUCE

YIELD: *10 to 12 scones*
BAKING TIME: *17 minutes*

BANANA CHOCOLATE CHIP MUFFINS I

YIELD: *12 muffins*
BAKING TIME: *20 minutes*

SCONES
2 cups all-purpose flour
⅓ cup granulated sugar
1½ teaspoons baking powder
½ cup finely ground almonds
¼ teaspoon salt
⅓ cup butter or margarine, cubed
½ cup sour cream or plain yogurt
1 large egg
1½ teaspoons almond extract
SAUCE
Chocolate Sauce III (see page 124)

1 Position a rack in the center of the oven and preheat the oven to 400 degrees. Lightly grease two baking sheets.

2 In a large bowl, combine the flour, sugar, baking powder, almonds, and salt. Using a pastry blender or two knives scissor fashion, cut in the butter to make a crumbly mixture.

3 In a medium bowl, using an electric mixer on high speed, beat the sour cream, egg, and almond extract until smooth.

4 Using a pastry blender or two knives, combine the flour mixture and the sour cream mixture and blend to make a soft, sticky dough. Drop the dough by heaping spoonfuls onto the prepared baking sheets, spacing them 2½ to 3 inches apart.

5 Bake for 15 to 17 minutes, or until a cake tester inserted into the center comes out clean. Invert onto a wire rack to cool completely.

6 Make the chocolate sauce.

7 Serve the muffins on individual dishes with the chocolate sauce spooned over the top.

1¼ cups plus 2 tablespoons all-purpose flour
⅓ cup granulated sugar
2 tablespoons Dutch processed unsweetened cocoa powder
1 tablespoon baking powder
1 cup mashed bananas (2 medium)
⅔ cup canola oil
1 large egg, beaten
1 cup semi-sweet chocolate chips

1 Position a rack in the center of the oven and preheat the oven to 425 degrees. Line twelve 2¼-inch muffin cups with paper baking cups.

2 In a large bowl, combine the flour, sugar, cocoa powder, and baking powder.

3 Blend the bananas, oil, and egg into the dry ingredients, mixing just until blended. Fold in the chocolate chips. Spoon the batter into the prepared muffin cups, filling them three-fourths full.

4 Bake for 15 to 20 minutes, or until a cake tester inserted into the center comes out clean. Cool in the muffins cups on a wire rack for several minutes. Invert onto the rack to cool completely.

Bishop's bread

YIELD: *2 loaves*
BAKING TIME: *1 hour*

2 cups all-purpose flour
1 cup granulated sugar
1 tablespoon baking powder
1 teaspoon salt
⅓ cup vegetable shortening
1½ cups orange juice
3 tablespoons canola oil
1 large egg
1 tablespoon grated orange zest
½ cup wheat germ
6 ounces semi-sweet chocolate,
   grated or finely chopped
¼ cup golden raisins
¼ cup candied cherry halves
¼ cup walnuts, chopped

1 Position a rack in the center of the oven and preheat the oven to 350 degrees. Lightly grease two 9 by 5-inch loaf pans.

2 In a large bowl, combine the flour, sugar, baking powder, and salt. Using a pastry blender or two knives scissor fashion, cut in the shortening into the dry ingredients to form a crumbly mixture.

3 In a medium bowl, combine the orange juice, oil, egg, and orange zest. Gradually blend into the dry ingredients. Add the wheat germ, chocolate, raisins, cherries, and nuts. Divide the mixture between the prepared pans and spread evenly.

4 Bake for 55 minutes to 1 hour, or until a cake tester inserted into the center comes out clean. Cool in the pans on a wire rack for 10 minutes. Invert onto the rack to cool completely.

Brunch coffee ring

YIELD: *10 to 12 servings*
BAKING TIME: *65 minutes*

COFFEE CAKE
2 cups all-purpose flour
1 teaspoon baking powder
1 teaspoon baking soda
½ teaspoon salt
1 cup sour cream
1 cup granulated sugar
2 large eggs
1 teaspoon Praline liqueur
½ cup semi-sweet chocolate chips
TOPPING
½ cup all-purpose flour
½ cup packed light brown sugar
1½ teaspoon Dutch processed cocoa
   powder
¼ cup butter or margarine, at room
   temperature
½ cup walnuts or pecans, chopped

1 Position a rack in the center of the oven and preheat the oven to 350 degrees. Lightly grease a 9-inch tube pan.

2 To make the cake, combine the flour, baking powder, baking soda, and salt.

3 In a large bowl, using an electric mixer on medium speed, beat the sour cream, sugar, eggs, and liqueur until combined. Gradually blend in the dry ingredients. Fold in the chocolate chips. Pour the mixture into the prepared pan and spread evenly.

4 To make the topping, in a medium bowl, combine the flour, brown sugar, and cocoa powder. Using a pastry blender or two knives scissor fashion, cut in the butter to form a crumbly mixture. Blend in the walnuts. Crumble the mixture over the batter in the pan.

5 Bake for 1 hour to 65 minutes, or until a cake tester inserted into the center comes out clean. Cool in the pan on a wire rack. Remove from the pan and place on a serving plate.

CHOCOLATE ALMOND TEA BREAD

YIELD: *2 loaves*
BAKING TIME: *55 minutes*

1¼ cups all-purpose flour
2½ cups whole wheat flour
2¼ teaspoons baking powder
½ teaspoon ground cinnamon
¼ teaspoon ground nutmeg
½ teaspoon salt
¼ cup butter or margarine, at room temperature
⅔ cup granulated sugar
2 large eggs
½ cup milk
¼ teaspoon almond or chocolate extract
½ cup sliced almonds
1 ounce semi-sweet chocolate, grated or finely chopped

1 Position a rack in the center of the oven and preheat the oven to 325 degrees. Lightly grease two 9 by 5-inch loaf pans.

2 Combine the flours, baking powder, cinnamon, nutmeg, and salt.

3 In a large bowl, using an electric mixer on medium speed, beat the butter and sugar until blended. Beat in the eggs, one at a time, beating well after each addition. Beat in milk and almond extract. Gradually blend in the dry ingredients. Fold in the almonds and grated chocolate. Divide the mixture between the prepared pans and spread evenly.

4 Bake for 50 to 55 minutes, or until a cake tester inserted into the center comes out clean. Cool in the pans on a wire rack.

BAKING NOTES: Each loaf makes 9 to 12 servings.

CHOCOLATE BREAKFAST CAKE WITH CHOCOLATE ALMOND SAUCE

YIELD: *10 to 12 servings*
RISING TIME: *2 hours*
BAKING TIME: *45 minutes*

2½ cups all-purpose flour
1½ cups granulated sugar
1 tablespoon active dry yeast
1 teaspoon baking soda
½ teaspoon salt
2 ounces unsweetened chocolate, grated or finely chopped
1 cup butter or margarine
1 cup milk
¼ cup Dutch processed cocoa powder
3 large eggs
1 cup Chocolate Almond Sauce I (see page 121)
¼ cup sliced almonds for garnish

1 Position a rack in the center of the oven and preheat the oven to 350 degrees. Lightly grease and flour a 10-inch Bundt pan.

2 Combine the flour, sugar, yeast, baking soda, and salt.

3 In the top of a double boiler over simmering water, melt the chocolate and butter, stirring until smooth. Stir in the milk and cocoa powder until smooth. Remove from the heat.

4 In a large bowl, using an electric mixer, beat the eggs until thick and light-colored. Pouring it in a thin stream, beat in the chocolate mixture. Gradually blend in the dry ingredients just until blended. Pour into the prepared pan. Cover with a towel and let rise for 2 hours, or until an indentation is left in the dough when poked.

5 Make the chocolate almond sauce.

6 Bake for 40 to 45 minutes, or until a cake tester inserted into the center comes out clean. Cool in the pan on a wire rack for 15 minutes. Invert onto a serving dish. Drizzle the chocolate almond sauce over the top of the cake, allowing it to drip down the sides, and sprinkle with sliced almonds. Serve warm.

CHOCOLATE CHERRY PECAN MUFFINS

YIELD: *12 muffins*
BAKING TIME: *25 minutes*

2 cups all-purpose flour
½ cup granulated sugar
1 cup Hershey's™ Chocolate Shoppe Candy Bar Sprinkles
1 cup chopped dried cherries
½ cup chopped pecans
1 tablespoon baking powder
½ teaspoon salt
1 cup milk
⅓ cup canola oil
⅓ cup butter or margarine, melted
1 large egg
12 whole pitted cherries, (canned)

1 Position a rack in the center of the oven and preheat the oven to 400 degrees. Lightly grease twelve 2¼-inch muffin cups.

2 Combine the flour, sugar, candy bar sprinkles, cherries, pecans, baking powder, and salt.

3 In a large bowl, using an electric mixer on high speed, beat the milk, oil, butter, and egg for 2 to 3 minutes, until smooth. Gradually blend in the dry ingredients, mixing just until incorporated. Spoon the batter into the prepared cups, filling them three-fourths full. Press 1 whole cherry into the center of each muffin.

4 Bake for 20 to 25 minutes, or until a cake tester inserted into the center comes out clean. Cool in the muffin cups on a wire rack for several minutes. Invert onto the rack to cool completely.

CHOCOLATE CHIP SCONES

YIELD: *8 to 12 scones*
BAKING TIME: *20 minutes*

½ cup buttermilk
1 large egg
1 teaspoon chocolate or vanilla extract
2 cups all-purpose flour
3 tablespoons granulated sugar
2 teaspoons baking powder
¼ teaspoon salt
½ cup butter or margarine
½ cup semi-sweet chocolate chips

1 Position a rack in the center of the oven and preheat the oven to 425 degrees. Lightly grease a baking sheet.

2 In a medium bowl, using an electric mixer on medium speed, beat the buttermilk, egg, and chocolate extract until combined.

3 In a large bowl, combine the flour, sugar, baking powder, and salt. Using a pastry blender or two knives scissor fashion, cut in the butter to form a crumbly mixture. Using a wooden spoon, stir in the buttermilk mixture. Fold in the chocolate chips, mixing until the mixture forms a soft dough.

4 On a lightly floured surface, knead the dough gently for 2 to 3 minutes. Roll out into an 8-inch circle. Using a sharp knife, score 8 to 12 wedges into the surface of the dough. Transfer to the prepared baking sheet.

5 Bake for 18 to 20 minutes, or until a cake tester inserted into the center comes out clean. Cool on the baking sheet on a wire rack for 5 minutes. Cut into wedges, and place on a serving plate. Serve warm.

Chocolate chip muffins I

YIELD: *12 muffins*
BAKING TIME: *20 minutes*

1 large egg
2 tablespoons butter or margarine,
   melted
¼ cup granulated sugar
2 ounces semi-sweet chocolate,
   grated or finely chopped
⅓ cup plus 1 tablespoon all-purpose
   flour
Pinch of salt

1 Position a rack in the center of
the oven and preheat the oven to
375 degrees. Line twelve 2¼-inch
muffin cups with paper baking cups.

2 In a medium bowl, using an
electric mixer on medium speed,
beat the egg until thick and light-
colored. Beat in butter and sugar.
Add the chocolate, flour, and salt
and blend just until moistened.
Spoon the batter into the prepared
muffin cups, filling them three-
fourths full.

3 Bake for 18 to 20 minutes, or
until a cake tester inserted into the
center comes out clean. Cool in the
muffin cups on a wire rack for several minutes. Invert onto the rack
to cool completely.

Chocolate chip zucchini bread

YIELD: *2 loaves*
BAKING TIME: *1 hour*

2 cups all-purpose flour
1 package (3.4 ounces) Jell-O Brand
   instant chocolate pudding mix
1 cup semi-sweet chocolate chips
½ cup shredded coconut
½ cup almonds, chopped
1 teaspoon baking powder
1 teaspoon ground cinnamon
1 teaspoon ground allspice
½ teaspoon salt
3 large eggs
1 cup granulated sugar
½ cup packed light-brown sugar
1 cup canola oil
1 tablespoon orange liqueur
2 cups grated zucchini
Powdered sugar for garnish

1 Position a rack in the center of
the oven and preheat the oven to
350 degrees. Lightly grease and
flour two 9 by 5-inch loaf pans.

2 Combine the flour, pudding mix,
chocolate chips, coconut, almonds,
baking powder, cinnamon, allspice,
and salt.

3 In a large bowl, using an electric
mixer on medium speed, beat the
eggs until thick and light-colored.
Beat in the sugars. Beat in the oil
and liqueur. Beat in the zucchini.
Gradually blend in the dry ingredients. Divide the mixture between
the prepared pans and spread evenly.

4 Bake for 55 minutes to 1 hour, or
until a cake tester inserted into the
center comes out clean. Cool in the
pans on a wire rack. Remove from
the pans and place on a serving plate.
Sprinkle with powdered sugar.

Chocolate date nut bread

Yield: *2 loaves*
baking time: *1 hour*

1½ cups all-purpose flour
½ cup Dutch processed cocoa powder
2 teaspoons ground cinnamon
1 teaspoon ground nutmeg
½ teaspoon ground allspice
1 teaspoon baking powder
½ teaspoon baking powder
¼ teaspoon salt
½ cup butter or margarine, at room temperature
1 cup granulated sugar
2 large eggs
1 cup buttermilk
1 cup (6 ounces) Hershey's™ Chocolate Shoppe Candy Bar Sprinkles
½ cup dates, pitted and finely chopped
½ cup pecans, coarsely chopped
1 recipe Rum Cream Frosting (see page 128)

1 Position a rack in the center of the oven and preheat the oven to 350 degrees. Grease two 9 by 5-inch loaf pans.

2 Combine the flour, cocoa powder, cinnamon, nutmeg, allspice, baking powder, baking soda, and salt.

3 In a large bowl, using an electric mixer on medium speed, beat the butter and sugar until smooth. Beat in the eggs, one at a time, beating well after each addition. In three additions, beat in the dry ingredients, alternating with the buttermilk, beginning and ending with the dry ingredients, mixing just until blended. Fold in the candy bar sprinkles, dates, and pecans. Divide the mixture between the prepared pans and spread evenly.

4 Bake for 55 minutes to 1 hour, or until a cake tester inserted into the center comes out clean. Cool in the pan on a wire rack for 5 minutes. Invert onto the rack to cool completely. Chill until ready to serve.

5 Make the frosting.

6 Place the cake on a serving plate. Spread the frosting over the top and sides of the cake and slice.

Baking notes: This is a very fragile cake and tends to fall apart if not kept well chilled.

CHOCOLATE FUDGE MUFFINS

YIELD: *12 muffins*
BAKING TIME: *45 minutes*

1½ cups granulated sugar
1 cup all-purpose flour
¼ teaspoon salt
4 ounces semi-sweet chocolate, grated or finely chopped
1 cup butter-flavored vegetable shortening
4 large eggs, beaten
1 teaspoon crème de cacao

1 Position a rack in the center of the oven and preheat the oven to 300 degrees. Line twelve 2¾-inch muffin cups with paper baking cups.

2 In a large bowl, combine the sugar, flour, and salt.

3 In the top of a double boiler over simmering water, melt the chocolate, stirring until smooth. Add the shortening and stir until melted. Remove from the heat. Beat in the eggs and crème de cacao and mix until cool. Add to the dry ingredients and mix just until blended. Spoon the mixture into the prepared muffin cups, filling them two-thirds full.

4 Bake for 40 to 45 minutes, or until a cake tester inserted into the center comes out clean. Cool in the pan on a wire rack for 5 minutes. Invert onto the rack to cool completely.

BAKING NOTES: These are simple little muffins, not the oversized puffy kind.

CHOCOLATE GINGERBREAD

YIELD: *12 to 15 servings*
BAKING TIME: *25 minutes*

2 cups all-purpose flour
2 teaspoons baking powder
¼ teaspoon baking soda
2 teaspoons ground cinnamon
1 teaspoon ground ginger
¼ teaspoon salt
1½ ounces unsweetened chocolate, grated or finely chopped
⅓ cup vegetable shortening
2 large eggs
¼ cup granulated sugar
¼ cup packed light-brown sugar
¼ cup dark molasses
½ cup milk
Powdered sugar for garnish

1 Position a rack in the center of the oven and preheat the oven to 350 degrees. Lightly grease a 13 by 9-inch baking pan.

2 Combine the flour, baking powder, baking soda, cinnamon, ginger, and salt.

3 In the top of a double boiler over simmering water, melt the chocolate and shortening, stirring until smooth. Remove from the heat. Beat in the eggs, one at a time. Beat in the sugars. Beat in the molasses and milk. Gradually blend in the dry ingredients. Pour the mixture into the prepared pan and spread evenly.

4 Bake for 20 to 25 minutes, or until a cake tester inserted into the center comes out clean. Cool in the pan on a wire rack. Remove from the pan and place on a serving plate. Sprinkle with powdered sugar and cut into squares.

CHOCOLATE NUT LOAVES

YIELD: *5 miniature loaves*
BAKING TIME: *40 minutes*

2¼ cups all-purpose flour
1 cup hazelnuts or pecans, chopped
3 tablespoons Dutch processed cocoa
  powder
1½ teaspoons baking powder
1 teaspoon baking soda
¼ teaspoon salt
1 cup butter-flavored vegetable
  shortening
2 cups granulated sugar
5 large eggs
1 cup buttermilk
1 tablespoon cider vinegar
2 teaspoons almond or chocolate
  extract

1 Position a rack in the center of the oven and preheat the oven to 350 degrees. Lightly grease five miniture loaf pans that are 5 by 3-inches.

2 Combine the flour, hazelnuts, cocoa powder, baking powder, baking soda, and salt.

3 In a large bowl, using an electric mixer on medium speed, beat the shortening and sugar until fluffy. Beat in the eggs, one at a time. Beat in the buttermilk, vinegar, and almond extract. Gradually blend in the dry ingredients. Divide the mixture between the prepared pans and spread evenly.

4 Bake for 30 to 40 minutes, or until a cake tester inserted into the center comes out clean. Cool in the pans on a wire rack.

BAKING NOTES: If you do not have miniature loaf pans, you can use two 9 by 5-inch loaf pans and increase the baking time by 10 to 15 minutes.

CHOCOLATE PANCAKES WITH CINNAMON CANDY WHIPPED CREAM

YIELD: *6 to 8 servings*

COCOA PANCAKES
1 large egg
1 cup milk
¼ cup canola oil
1¼ cups all-purpose flour
6 tablespoons Dutch processed cocoa powder
¼ cup plus 2 tablespoons granulated sugar
2 teaspoons baking powder
¾ teaspoon salt

CINNAMON CANDY WHIPPED CREAM
1½ cups heavy cream
2 tablespoons granulated sugar
1 teaspoon chocolate or vanilla extract
¼ cup cinnamon candies, crushed

1 Preheat a griddle or skillet over medium-high heat until a drop of water sizzles when dropped onto the pan.

2 In a small bowl, beat the egg until foamy. Beat in the milk and oil.

3 In a large bowl, combine the flour, cocoa powder, sugar, baking powder, and salt. Gradually blend in the egg mixture just until moistened.

4 Brush the griddle with oil. Spoon about 1½ tablespoons of the batter onto the prepared griddle. Cook until holes start to appear around the edges and the top starts to look dry. Turn and brown on the other side. Do not overcook. Place on a wire rack until ready to serve.

5 To make the whipped cream, in a medium bowl, using an electric mixer on high speed, whip the cream, sugar, and chocolate extract until soft peaks form. Fold in the candy until well blended.

6 To serve, place three pancakes on each plate, placing a dab of the whipped cream between each one and an additional dab on the top.

BAKING NOTES: Any flavor of hard candy can be used. The candy can be finely crushed into a powder or left in larger pieces. Substitute any liqueur or brandy for the chocolate extract.

Chocolate oat scones

Yield: *8 scones*
BAKING TIME: *18 minutes*

1 cup all-purpose flour
¼ cup packed light-brown sugar
¼ cup Dutch processed cocoa powder
1½ teaspoons baking powder
¼ teaspoon baking soda
¼ teaspoon salt
3 tablespoons butter or margarine, at room temperature
½ cup old-fashioned oats
½ cup dried cherries or cranberries
2 large eggs
¼ cup buttermilk

1 Position a rack in the center of the oven and preheat the oven to 400 degrees. Lightly grease a baking sheet.

2 In a large bowl, combine the flour, brown sugar, cocoa powder, baking powder, baking soda, and salt. Using a pastry blender or two knives scissor fashion, cut in the butter to form a crumbly mixture. Using a wooden spoon, stir in the oats and cherries. Stir in the eggs and just enough buttermilk to make a smooth, workable dough.

3 On a lightly floured surface, roll the dough out to create an 8-inch round circle. Transfer to the prepared baking sheet, and using a serrated knife, cut the circle into 8 wedges.

4 Bake for 16 to 18 minutes, or until a cake tester inserted into the center comes out clean.

5 Cool on the baking sheet on a wire rack and place on a serving plate.

CHOCOLATE ORANGE BREAKFAST LOAF

YIELD: *1 loaf*
BAKING TIME: *1 hour*

CHOCOLATE ORANGE CAKE
2 ounces unsweetened chocolate,
   grated or finely chopped
1¼ cups all-purpose flour
¾ teaspoon baking powder
¾ teaspoon baking soda
1 cup butter or margarine, at room
   temperature
1 cup granulated sugar
1 teaspoon orange or vanilla extract
3 large eggs
1 cup sour cream
1 tablespoon grated orange zest
1 teaspoon chocolate or
   vanilla extract

GRAND MARNIER GLAZE
⅓ cup Grand Marnier
3 tablespoons powdered sugar

1 Position a rack in the center of the oven and preheat the oven to 350 degrees. Lightly grease and flour a 9 by 5-inch loaf pan.

2 To make the cake, melt the chocolate (see page ●●●). Remove from the heat.

3 Combine the flour, baking powder, and baking soda.

4 In a large bowl, using an electric mixer on medium speed, beat the butter and sugar until smooth. Beat in the vanilla extract. Beat in the eggs, one at a time, beating well after each addition. Blend in the dry ingredients. Beat in the sour cream. Place half of the batter in another bowl. Add the orange zest to the first bowl and mix. Pour the batter into the prepared pan and spread evenly.

5 In a medium bowl, mix the melted chocolate and chocolate extract. Gently spread chocolate mixture over orange flavored batter.

6 Bake for 55 minutes to 1 hour, or until a cake tester inserted into the center comes out clean. Cool in the pan on a wire rack for 5 minutes. Invert onto a wire rack to cool completely.

7 To make the glaze, in a small saucepan, over low heat, combine the Grand Marnier and powdered sugar. Raise the temperature to medium and bring to a boil. Simmer for 1 minute. Remove from the heat and spoon over the top of the cake.

CHOCOLATE WAFFLES II
YIELD: *4 to 6 servings*

COCOA BREAD
YIELD: *1 loaf*
BAKING TIME: *55 minutes*

2 cups all-purpose flour
¼ cup granulated sugar
3 tablespoons Dutch processed cocoa powder
1 tablespoon baking powder
¼ teaspoon salt
1¼ cups milk
¼ cup butter, or margarine melted
2 large eggs
1 teaspoon crème de cacao or chocolate extract
Syrup or fruit in season for serving
Whipped cream for garnish

1 Preheat a waffle iron.

2 Combine the flour, sugar, cocoa powder, baking powder, and salt.

3 In the container of a blender, combine the milk, butter, eggs, and crème de cacao and blend for a few seconds. On low speed, gradually blend in the dry ingredients until well mixed.

4 Pour the batter onto the preheated waffle iron, using about ¾ cup for each waffle. Close and bake according to the manufacturer's directions. Serve hot with syrup or fruit in season and garnish with whipped cream.

1¼ cups all-purpose flour
¼ cup Dutch processed cocoa powder
¾ teaspoon allspice
¼ teaspoon baking powder
⅛ teaspoon baking soda
½ teaspoon salt
2 large eggs
¾ cup packed light-brown sugar
¾ cup sour cream or chocolate yogurt
¼ cup butter or margarine, melted
Cocoa Sugar (see page 125) for garnish

1 Position a rack in the center of the oven and preheat the oven to 375 degrees. Lightly grease a 9 by 5-inch loaf pan.

2 Combine the flour, cocoa powder, allspice, baking powder, baking soda, and salt.

3 In a large bowl, using an electric mixer on high speed, beat the eggs until light-colored. Beat in the brown sugar, sour cream, and butter. Gradually mix in the dry ingredients just until blended. Do not overmix. Pour the mixture into the prepared pan and spread evenly.

4 Bake for 50 to 55 minutes, or until a cake tester inserted into the center comes out clean. Cool in the pan on a wire rack for 10 minutes. Invert onto the rack to cool completely. Sprinkle with cocoa sugar.

CRÊPES WITH CHOCOLATE SAUCE

YIELD: *12 to 14 crêpes*
CHILL TIME: *2 hours*

⅔ cup all-purpose flour
1 tablespoon granulated sugar
Pinch of salt
2 large eggs
1⅓ cups milk
2 tablespoons butter or margarine, melted
1 tablespoon coffee liqueur
1 cup Chocolate Sauce III (see page 124)
Melted butter for brushing pan
1 cup apricot jam
Fresh pansies for garnish

1 Combine the flour, sugar, and salt.

2 In a large bowl, using an electric mixer on medium speed, beat the eggs until thick and light-colored. On low speed, beat in the milk. Gradually, blend in the dry ingredients. Stir in the melted butter and coffee liqueur. Cover and chill for 2 hours.

3 Make the chocolate sauce.

4 Brush the bottom of the crêpe pan or small skillet with butter and heat over medium heat. Pour about ¼ cup of the chilled batter into the pan and use the back of a spoon to spread it out as thinly as possible. Cook for about 1 minutes on each side. Transfer to a plate and keep warm.

5 To serve, spread each crêpe with a layer of apricot jam and roll up loosely. Place on serving plates and spoon the chocolate sauce over the top. Garnish with pansies.

BAKING NOTES: **Two crêpes can be cooked at once if a large skillet is used.**

DOUBLE CHOCOLATE MUFFINS I

YIELD: *12 muffins*
BAKING TIME: *20 minutes*

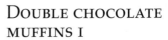

2 cups all-purpose flour
1½ cups miniature chocolate chips
¼ cup Dutch processed cocoa powder
1 tablespoon baking powder
½ cup vegetable shortening
1 cup granulated sugar
1 large egg
1 cup milk

1 Position a rack in the center of the oven and preheat the oven to 400 degrees. Lightly grease twelve 2¾-inch muffin cups.

2 Combine the flour, chocolate chips, cocoa powder, and baking powder.

3 In a large bowl, using an electric mixer on medium speed, beat the shortening and sugar until fluffy. Beat in the egg. Beat in the milk. Blend in the dry ingredients, stirring until just moistened. Spoon the batter into the prepared muffin cups, filling them three-fourths full.

4 Bake for 18 to 20 minutes, or until a cake tester inserted into the center comes out clean. Cool in the muffin cups on a wire rack for several minutes. Invert onto the rack to cool completely.

CHOCOLATE FILLED BREAKFAST ROLL

YIELD: *10 to 12 servings*
BAKING TIME: *30 minutes*

ROLLS
1 envelope active dry yeast
¼ cup warm water (105 to 110 degrees)
2½ cups all-purpose flour
½ cup Dutch processed cocoa powder
1¼ cups granulated sugar
¼ teaspoon salt
¼ cup butter or margarine, at room temperature
3 large eggs

FILLING
2 ounces unsweetened chocolate, grated or finely chopped
½ cup honey
2 tablespoon Frangelico or amaretto
2 cups ground hazelnuts
½ cup black currants
Grand Marnier Sauce (see page 127) for serving

1 Position a rack in the lower third of the oven and preheat the oven to 375 degrees. Lightly grease a baking sheet or jelly roll pan.

2 In a cup, sprinkle the yeast over the warm water and set aside.

3 In a large bowl, combine the flour, cocoa powder, sugar, and salt. Using a pastry blender or two knives scissor fashion, cut in the butter. Using an electric mixer on medium speed, beat in eggs, one at a time, beating well after each addition. Blend in the yeast and form a smooth dough. On a lightly floured surface, knead for 2 to 3 minutes. Place in a buttered or floured bowl and let rise for up to 2 hours, until doubled in bulk.

4 To make the filling, melt the chocolate (see page •••). Remove from the heat. Using an electric mixer on low speed, beat in the Frangelico. Using a spoon or spatula, fold in the hazelnuts and currants until combined.

5 On a lightly floured surface, roll out the dough to a thickness of ½ inch. Spread the filling evenly over the dough, leaving a ½-inch border on the edges. Using a pastry brush, lightly brush the border with water and roll up the dough, jelly-roll fashion. Seal the seam and ends by pinching them together. Place in the center of the prepared baking sheet.

6 Bake for 25 to 30 minutes, or until a cake tester inserted on the edges (not filling) comes out clean. Cool on a wire rack. Serve with Grand Marnier sauce on the side.

Hazelnut scones

Yield: *8 scones*
baking time: *20 minutes*

1 cup all-purpose flour
1 cup whole wheat flour
⅓ cup packed light brown sugar
1½ teaspoons baking powder
½ teaspoon baking soda
¼ teaspoon salt
6 tablespoons butter or margarine
½ cup buttermilk
1 large egg
1½ teaspoons hazelnut liqueur
6 ounces semi-sweet chocolate,
    grated or finely chopped
½ cup hazelnuts, chopped
Jam or jelly for serving

1 Position a rack in the center of the oven and preheat the oven to 400 degrees. Lightly grease a baking sheet.

2 In a large bowl, combine the flours, brown sugar, baking powder, baking soda, and salt. Using a pastry blender or two knives scissor fashion, cut in the butter to form a crumbly mixture.

3 In a small bowl, using an electric mixer on medium speed, beat the buttermilk, egg, and liqueur. Gradually blend into the dry mixture, stirring just until moistened. Fold in the grated chocolate and hazelnuts.

4 On a floured surface, roll out the dough to a thickness of ½ inch. Using a 2 to 2½-inch round cookie cutter, cut out as many rounds as possible. Place the rounds on the prepared baking sheet, spacing them 1 inch apart.

5 Bake for 17 to 20 minutes, or until a cake test inserted into the center comes out clean. Cool on the baking sheet on a wire rack for 5 minutes. Invert onto the rack to cool completely. Serve warm or cold with jam or jelly on the side.

Baking notes: As an alternative, sprinkle with cocoa sugar (see page 125). Or, using dipping chocolate (see page 126), dip half of each scone in chocolate when cool.

Mud pie scones

Yield: *8 to 10 scones*
baking time: *18 minutes*

2 cups all-purpose flour
½ cup packed light-brown sugar
⅓ cup Dutch processed cocoa powder
2½ teaspoons baking powder
¼ teaspoon salt
⅓ cup butter or margarine
½ cup chocolate yogurt
1 tablespoon water
1 large egg
1 teaspoon chocolate or
    vanilla extract
Jam or jelly for serving

1 Position a rack in the center of the oven and preheat the oven to 375 degrees. Lightly grease two baking sheets.

2 In a large bowl, combine the flour, brown sugar, cocoa powder, baking powder, and salt. Using a pastry blender or two knives scissor fashion, cut in the butter to form a crumbly mixture.

3 In a medium bowl, using an electric mixer on high speed, beat the yogurt, water, egg, and chocolate extract until well blended. Stir into the flour mixture to form a soft sticky dough. Drop the dough by heaping spoonfuls onto the prepared baking sheet, spacing them 2½ to 3 inches apart.

4 Bake for 16 to 18 minutes, or until a cake tester inserted into the center comes out clean. Invert onto a wire rack to cool for 5 minutes. Serve warm with jam or jelly.

Ricotta cheese-filled cream puffs

YIELD: *12 servings*
BAKING TIME: *1 hour*

CREAM PUFF PASTRY
1 cup water
½ cup butter or margarine
¼ teaspoon salt
1 cup all-purpose flour
4 large eggs
RICOTTA FILLING
1 pound ricotta cheese
¼ cup granulated sugar
**2 ounces semi-sweet chocolate,
  grated or finely chopped**
3 tablespoons evaporated milk
**1 teaspoon chocolate or
  vanilla extract**
CHOCOLATE FROSTING
**Chocolate Fudge Frosting II
  (see page 123)**

1 Position a rack in the center of the oven and preheat the oven to 375 degrees. Lightly grease two baking sheets.

2 In a large saucepan, over medium heat, heat the water, butter, and salt until the butter is melted. Raise the temperature to high. Bring to a boil and immediately remove from the heat.

3 Add the flour and return to the heat. Stir for about 1 minute with a wooden spoon until the mixture leaves the side of the pan and forms a ball. Remove from the heat. Beat in the eggs, one at a time, mixing well after each addition. Drop the dough by heaping spoonfuls onto the prepared baking sheets, making twelve mounds spaced 3 inches apart.

4 Bake for 50 minutes. Remove from the oven and immediately cut a small slit into the side of the each puff. Return to the oven and bake for 10 minutes or until a cake tester inserted into the sides (not in the cheese filling) comes out clean. Invert onto a wire rack to cool. Cover and chill until ready to use.

5 To make the filling, in a small bowl, using an electric mixer on high speed, beat the ricotta cheese, sugar, chocolate, 1 tablespoon of the milk, and the chocolate extract. Add the remaining milk, a little at a time, until it is the consistency of thick mayonnaise. Cover and chill until ready to use.

6 Make the frosting.

7 To assemble, using a small serrated knife, cut the puffs horizontally halfway through, leaving just enough pastry on one side to act as a hinge. Fill each of the puffs with some of the filling. Spread a spoonful of the frosting over the top. Chill for at least 1 hour before serving.

BAKING NOTES: An alternative method of filling the cream puffs is to use a pastry bag. Fill a pastry bag fitted with a large round tip with the filling and pipe it through the slit made in the puffs while baking.

TRIPLE CHOCOLATE MUFFINS

YIELD: *12 muffins*
BAKING TIME: *35 minutes*

1 cup all-purpose flour
3 tablespoons Dutch processed cocoa
   powder
Pinch of salt
1 cup butter or margarine
2 ounces unsweetened chocolate,
   grated or finely chopped
2 ounces semi-sweet chocolate,
   grated or finely chopped
1½ cups granulated sugar
4 large eggs
1 teaspoon crème de cacao
12 pecan halves

1 Position a rack in the center of the oven and preheat the oven to 350 degrees. Lightly grease twelve 2¼-inch muffin cups or line them with paper baking cups.

2 Combine the flour, cocoa powder, and salt.

3 In the top of a double boiler over simmering water, melt the butter and chocolates, stirring until smooth. Remove from the heat and stir in the sugar. Using an electric mixer on medium speed, beat in the eggs, one at a time. Beat in the crème de cacao. Gradually blend in the dry ingredients. Spoon the bat-ter into the prepared muffin cups, filling them to the top. Press a pecan half into each cup.

4 Bake for 30 to 35 minutes, or until a cake tester inserted into the center comes out clean. Invert onto a wire rack to cool.

BAKING NOTES: It is very easy to over-bake these muffins. If you do, they will be dry.

ALMOND CRUST

YIELD: *on 9-inch pie crust*
FREEZING TIME: *30 minutes*

1¾ cups almonds, coarsely ground
3 tablespoons butter-flavored
   vegetable shortening
2 tablespoons light corn syrup

1 Lightly grease a 9-inch pie pan.

2 In a medium bowl, combine the almonds, shortening, and corn syrup. Press the mixture onto the bottom and up the sides of the prepared pie pan. Cover and freeze for 30 minutes, or until ready to fill.

APRICOT ROSES

YIELD: *1 rose*
FREEZING TIME: *30 minutes*

7 dried apricot halves
½ cup apricot liqueur
Chocolate Leaves (see page 128)

1 In a small bowl, place the apricot halves and pour the liqueur over them. Soak for at least 1 hour.

2 Drain, reserving the liquid for another use. Lightly pat the apricots dry with paper towels. Place one of the halves between two sheets of waxed paper. Using a rolling pin, roll out the half as thinly as possible. Repeat with the remaining apricot halves.

3 To form a flower, roll one of the flattened apricot halves around itself to make a very tight cylinder. To add petals, place another apricot half against the cylinder and pinch at the base to make it stick. Repeat with the remaining apricot halves until a rose in full bloom is formed.

4 Insert a wooden toothpick into the base of the cylinder and trim the bottom of the flower as necessary. Curl the outside tips of each petal. Place on a baking sheet and freeze for 30 minutes, or until firm.

5 Place the rose on a frosted cake and brush the petal tips with water. Dust the rose with coarse granulated sugar or sugar crystals. Arrange chocolate leaves around the flower using small amounts of moist frosting as an adhesive.

BAKING NOTES: For best results, roll out the apricot halves as thinly as possible. Other dried fruits can also be used. Dried peaches make paler-colored roses. Purchased fruit leather can also be used and has the advantage of being paper-thin. Craft books on artificial flower making will have patterns for rose petals that can be used with the fruit leather.

CHOCOLATE ALMOND SAUCE I

YIELD: *1¼ cups*

1 can (12 ounces) evaporated milk
½ cup granulated sugar
¼ cup Dutch processed cocoa powder
2 teaspoons cornstarch
1 teaspoon almond extract

1 In a medium saucepan, over medium heat, combine the milk, sugar, cocoa powder, and cornstarch, stirring constantly until smooth. Bring to a boil. Remove from the heat.

2 Stir in the almond extract. Using an electric mixer on medium speed, beat until the mixture cools to room temperature. Serve cool or lukewarm. Chill any unused portion in the refrigerator.

CHOCOLATE COCONUT FROSTING

YIELD: *2½ to 3 cups*

¾ cup heavy cream
½ cup granulated sugar
⅓ cup coconut liqueur
1 tablespoon cornstarch or arrowroot
1 large egg yolk, beaten
3 ounces unsweetened chocolate,
   grated or finely chopped
3 ounces semi-sweet chocolate,
   grated or finely chopped
2 tablespoons butter or margarine
1⅓ cups flaked coconut
1 cup chopped almonds or pecans
1 teaspoon almond or chocolate
   extract

1 In a large saucepan, over medium-low heat, combine the cream, sugar, liqueur, cornstarch, and egg yolk, stirring constantly, until well blended and smooth. Cook for 5 to 7 minutes, or until the mixture thickens. Remove from the heat and stir in the chocolates, butter, coconut, almonds, and almond extract. Cool until a spreadable consistency.

CHOCOLATE COOKIE CRUMB CRUST

YIELD: *one 9-inch pie crust*
BAKING TIME: *10 minutes*

1½ cups chocolate wafer cookie crumbs
¼ cup butter or margarine, at room temperature
1 tablespoon chocolate extract

1 Position a rack in the center of the oven and preheat the oven to 375 degrees.

2 In a medium bowl, combine the cookie crumbs, butter, and chocolate extract. Using your fingertips, a pastry blender, or a fork, add the butter into the crumbs until thoroughly blended. Press the mixture into a 9-inch pie pan.

3 Bake for 8 to 10 minutes, or until the crust looks dry. Cool completely on a wire rack.

BAKING NOTES: This crust can be made with almost any kind of cookie crumbs.

CHOCOLATE CURLS

CHILL TIME: *30 minutes*

Semi-sweet, milk, or white chocolate bars

1 Line a baking sheet with waxed or parchment paper.

2 Dip the blade of a sharp vegetable peeler in hot water and wipe dry. Grasp the chocolate with a paper towel so that the heat from your hand does not melt the chocolate. Scrape the vegetable peeler along one of the edges in a downward motion to form tight curls, letting them fall onto the prepared pan. Warm the blade again in hot water, if necessary. Cover and chill the curls 30 minutes, or until using. Use the top of a knife or a pair of tweezers to handle the curls.

BAKING NOTES: There are many ways to make chocolate curls. This method is easiest for the home baker. If the chocolate is too cold, it will form shavings rather than curls. If this happens, warm the surface of the chocolate a little by placing your hand on it. If it is too warm, strips of chocolate rather than curls are formed. A melon baller can also be used. The harder you scrape the chocolate the more open the curl will be.

CHOCOLATE CUSTARD SAUCE

YIELD: *2½ to 3 cups*
CHILL TIME: *30 minutes*

4 large egg yolks
¼ cup powdered sugar
2 cups milk
⅛ teaspoon salt
2 ounces unsweetened chocolate, grated or finely chopped
1 tablespoon crème de cacao

1 In a medium bowl, using an electric mixer on high speed, beat the egg yolks and sugar until thick and light-colored. Beat in the milk and salt.

2 Place the mixture in the top of a double boiler set over simmering water and cook, stirring frequently, until the mixture thickens and coats the back of a spoon. Remove from the heat and mix in the chocolate until smooth. Stir in the crème de cacao. Cover and chill for 30 minutes.

CHOCOLATE CUTOUTS

YIELD: *1 cup*
CHILL TIME: *30 minutes*

1 cup semi-sweet chocolate chips
2 tablespoons vegetable shortening

1 Line a baking sheet with aluminum foil, wax, or parchment paper.

2 In the top of a double boiler over simmering water, melt the chocolate and shortening, stirring until smooth. Pour the mixture onto the prepared pan and spread out to a thickness of ¼ inch. Cool until set but not hardened. The chocolate should not be allowed to harden and become brittle.

3 Use cookie cutters or a stencil and a sharp knife to cut out the desired shapes. Transfer the cutouts to a waxed paper-lined baking sheet ½-inch apart and cool completely. Cover and chill 30 minutes, or until using.

BAKING NOTES: Semi-sweet chocolate or white chocolate can be substituted for the chocolate chips. When a cookie cutter is not available, draw the design on paper or cardboard and cut out. Use it as a stencil and cut out the shape in the chocolate with a sharp, heavy knife.

CHOCOLATE FROSTING V
YIELD: *1 cup*

2 ounces unsweetened chocolate, grated or finely chopped
½ cup boiling water
½ cup butter or margarine, at room temperature
2 cups powdered sugar

1 In the container of a blender, combine the chocolate, boiling water, and butter. Blend on medium speed for 2 to 3 seconds, or until smooth. Add 1 cup of the powdered sugar and blend until smooth. Add the remaining 1 cup powdered sugar and blend until creamy.

CHOCOLATE FUDGE FROSTING II
YIELD: *1½ to 2 cups*

½ cup butter or margarine
2 ounces unsweetened chocolate, grated or finely chopped
1¾ cups granulated sugar
½ cup heavy cream
1 tablespoon dark corn syrup
1 teaspoon chocolate or vanilla extract

1 In a saucepan over low heat, melt the butter and chocolate, stirring until smooth. Mix in the sugar, cream, and corn syrup and bring to a boil. Cook for 3 minutes, stirring constantly. Remove from the heat and cool for 7 minutes. Add the chocolate extract and beat until a spreadable consistency.

CHOCOLATE FUDGE SAUCE
YIELD: *1 to 1½ cups*

6 ounces semi-sweet chocolate, grated or finely chopped
1 tablespoon butter or margarine
¼ cup hot water
¼ cup granulated sugar
¼ cup dark corn syrup
1 teaspoon chocolate extract or crème de cacao

1 In the top of a double boiler over simmering water, melt the chocolate and butter with the water, stirring until smooth. Add the sugar and stir until completely dissolved. Remove from the heat and stir in the corn syrup and chocolate extract. Serve warm.

CHOCOLATE GLAZE IV
YIELD: *1½ to 2 cups*

8 ounces unsweetened chocolate, grated or finely chopped
4 ounces semi-sweet chocolate, grated or finely chopped
6 tablespoons warm water (102 to 115 degrees)

1 In the top of a double boiler over simmering water, melt the chocolates, stirring until smooth. Remove from the heat. Add the water and beat until it is the consistency of heavy cream. Use at room temperature.

BAKING NOTES: If the glaze is too thick, add water, a teaspoon at a time.

CHOCOLATE HAZELNUT CRUMB CRUST
YIELD: *one 9-inch pie crust*

1¼ cups chocolate wafer cookie crumbs
¼ cup finely ground hazelnuts
3 tablespoons sugar
6 tablespoons butter or margarine, melted

1 In a medium bowl, combine the cookie crumbs, hazelnuts, and sugar. Using a fork, blend in the melted butter. Press the mixture evenly onto the bottom and up the sides of a 9-inch pie pan. Cover with waxed paper, weigh down with dry beans or pie weights, and freeze until ready to use.

BAKING NOTES: Any kind of nut can be used in place of the hazelnuts.

CHOCOLATE PIE SHELL

YIELD: *one 9-inch pie shell*
CHILL TIME: *2 hours*

12 ounces semi-sweet chocolate, grated or finely chopped
2 tablespoons butter or margarine
2 tablespoons granulated sugar

1 In the top of a double boiler over simmering water, melt the chocolate and butter, stirring until smooth. Stir in the sugar until dissolved. Immediately pour the mixture into a 9-inch foil pie pan, tipping and using a spoon to spread the chocolate up the sides. Chill for at least 1 hour, or until firm.

2 Carefully invert the pan onto a plate to remove the chocolate shell. Then reinvert onto a serving plate. Chill for 1 hour, or until ready to fill.

3 Fill with mousse or light custard pie filling.

BAKING NOTES: This pie shell will chip and crack very easily. Let stand at room temperature for at least 30 minutes before serving to soften it. In warmer weather, reduce the time out of the refrigerator.

CHOCOLATE PASTRY CRUST

YIELD: *one 9-inch pie crust*
BAKING TIME: *8 minutes*

1 cup all-purpose flour
¼ Cup Dutch processed cocoa powder
3 tablespoons sugar
¼ teaspoon salt
½ cup butter-flavored vegetable shortening
1 teaspoon chocolate or vanilla extract
2 tablespoons ice water

1 Position a rack in the center of the oven and preheat the oven to 400 degrees.

2 In a large bowl, combine the flour, cocoa powder, sugar, and salt. Using a pastry blender or two knives scissor fashion, cut in the shortening until the mixture forms coarse crumbs. Blend in the chocolate extract. Sprinkle the water over the top and mix gently with a fork just until moist enough to hold together.

3 On a lightly floured surface, roll the dough out into a circle 10 inches in diameter and about ¼ inch thick. Transfer to a 9-inch pie pan and ease into the bottom and up the sides. Trim the edges and flute if desired. Prick all over with a fork.

4 Bake for 8 minutes, or until the crust is slightly firm to the touch and looks dry.

CHOCOLATE RUM ICING

YIELD : *1½ cups*

3 ounces semi-sweet chocolate, grated or finely chopped
5 cups powdered sugar
6 tablespoons dark rum
2 tablespoons crème de cacao

1 Melt the chocolate (see page ●●●). Remove from the heat and transfer to a medium bowl.

2 Using an electric mixer on medium speed, beat in the powdered sugar and rum. Add the crème de cacao and beat until a spreadable consistency.

CHOCOLATE SAUCE III

YIELD: *2 to 2¼ cups*

1 teaspoon cornstarch or arrowroot
¾ cup heavy cream
6 ounces semi-sweet chocolate, grated or finely chopped
½ cup honey

1 In a small bowl, dissolve the cornstarch in the cream.

2 In the top of a double boiler over simmering water, melt the chocolate with the honey, stirring until smooth. Blend in the cream mixture and cook, stirring, until the sauce is thickened. Cool before using.

CHOCOLATE SAUCE V

YIELD : *1 to 1½ cup*

1 cup granulated sugar
½ cup water
2 ounces semi-sweet chocolate, grated or finely chopped
1 teaspoon chocolate or vanilla extract

1 In the top of a double boiler over simmering water, combine the sugar, water, and chocolate, stirring until smooth. Remove from the heat and stir in the chocolate extract. The sauce will be thin. Cool to room temperature before serving.

Chocolate sauce VIII

YIELD : 3/4 cup

1 cup granulated sugar
1/3 cup Dutch processed cocoa powder
1/4 teaspoon salt
1/2 cup warm water
1/4 cup light corn syrup
2 tablespoons butter or margarine
1 teaspoon chocolate or
    vanilla extract

1 In a medium saucepan, over low heat, combine the sugar, cocoa powder, and salt. Stir in the water and corn syrup until smooth. Insert a candy thermometer and cook until 234 degrees, stirring occasionally. Remove from the heat and stir in the butter and chocolate extract. Serve warm or cold over ice cream, cake, or fresh fruit.

Chocolate syrup I

YIELD : 1 1/2 to 2 cups

5 ounces unsweetened chocolate,
    grated or finely chopped
1 1/3 cups hot water
1 cup granulated sugar
1 teaspoon chocolate or
    vanilla extract

1 In the top of a double boiler over simmering water, melt the chocolate with the water, stirring until blended and smooth. Add the sugar and cook for 3 to 5 minutes, or until the sugar is dissolved. Remove from the heat and stir in the chocolate extract. Serve either warm or cold.

Chocolate syrup II

YIELD : 1 1/4 to 1 1/2 cups

3 ounces unsweetened chocolate,
    grated or finely chopped
2/3 cup water
1/2 cup granulated sugar
1/2 cup light or dark corn syrup
1/2 teaspoon chocolate or vanilla
    extract

1 In a saucepan over low heat, melt the chocolate with the water, stirring until smooth and thick. Stir in the sugar. Bring to a boil and simmer for 2 minutes. Add the corn syrup and return to a boil. Remove from the heat and cool slightly. Stir in the chocolate extract and cool completely.

Chocolate whipped cream

YIELD: 2 to 2 1/2 cups
CHILL TIME: 30 minutes

3 tablespoons powdered sugar
2 tablespoons Dutch processed
    cocoa powder
1 cup heavy cream
1/2 teaspoon crème de cacao

1 In a cup, combine the powdered sugar and cocoa powder.

2 In a medium bowl, using an electric mixer on high speed, whip the cream until soft peaks form. Fold in the dry ingredients. Fold in the crème de cacao. Chill for 30 minutes before using.

Cocoa sugar

YIELD: 1 cup

1 cup powdered sugar
1 tablespoon Dutch processed cocoa
    powder

1 In a small bowl, combine the powdered sugar and cocoa powder. Use for dusting over baked goods.

Coconut pie crust

YIELD: one 9-inch pie crust
BAKING TIME: 10 minutes

2 cups flaked coconut
2 tablespoons powdered sugar
1 tablespoon cornstarch
3 tablespoons butter or margarine
    melted

1 Position a rack in the center of the oven and preheat the oven to 350 degrees.

2 In a medium bowl, combine the coconut, powdered sugar, and cornstarch. Stir in the melted butter until thoroughly mixed. Press onto the bottom and up the sides of a 9-inch pie pan.

3 Bake for 8 to 10 minutes, or until lightly browned. Cool completely on a wire rack.

BAKING NOTES: Use flaked rather than shredded or grated coconut for a finer textured crust. The crust can be tinted with a few drops of food coloring, but take into consideration the color of the filling.

COFFEE MOCHA ICING

YIELD: *1 cup*

¾ cup powdered sugar
5 tablespoons milk
Pinch of salt
¼ cup butter or margarine
2 teaspoons mocha-flavored instant coffee powder
1 teaspoon chocolate or vanilla extract

1 In a large bowl, mix the powdered sugar, milk, and salt until smooth.

2 In a small saucepan, over low heat, melt the butter with the coffee powder, stirring until smooth. Stir in the chocolate extract. Remove from the heat. Gradually blend in the powdered sugar mixture and continue to cook, stirring occasionally, for 30 minutes, or until a spreadable consistency. If too thick, add a little more milk. If too thin, cook a little longer.

CUSTARD FILLING

YIELD: *¾ to 1 cup*
CHILL TIME: *30 minutes*

1 large egg
¾ cup skim milk
2 tablespoons powdered sugar
1 tablespoon cornstarch or arrowroot
Pinch of salt

1 In a small bowl, beat the egg.

2 In a medium saucepan, over medium heat, combine the milk, powdered sugar, cornstarch, and salt over medium heat. Stir constantly with a wire whisk until thickened and bubbly. Remove from the heat. Beat 2 tablespoons of the hot milk mixture into the beaten egg. Add the egg mixture to the saucepan, whisking constantly. Over medium-low heat, cook, stirring constantly, for 2 minutes. Transfer to a small bowl. Cover and chill 30 minutes, or until using.

DESSERT SYRUP

YEILD: *⅓ to ½ cup*

½ cup granulated sugar
2 tablespoons liqueur of choice

1 In a cup, combine the ingredients and mix until smooth. Use a pastry brush to brush over fruit on cakes and pies.

DIPPING CHOCOLATE

YIELD: *2 pounds*

2 pounds semi-sweet chocolate, grated or finely chopped

1 In the top of a double boiler, over hot, but not boiling water, melt the chocolate, stirring constantly until smooth. When the chocolate is melted, insert a chocolate thermometer, immersing the bulb completely. Stir the chocolate frequently, using a rapid circular motion, until the thermometer temperature reaches 110 degrees. Remove the top of the double boiler. Replace the hot water with cold tap water and replace the top of the double boiler. Stir the chocolate frequently, until the thermometer temperature drops to 83 degrees. Be sure to scrape down the sides of the pan as you stir.

2 Remove the top of the double boiler and check the temperature of the water with the thermometer. Add enough hot water, a little at a time, to bring the temperature up to 85 degrees. Wipe the thermometer clean and replace it in the chocolate. The chocolate is now tempered and ready for dipping candies.

3 Dip candies into the chocolate on a bamboo skewer or a fondue fork. Dip each candy deep into the chocolate, using a circular motion. Let the excess chocolate drip off and place the chocolate-coated candy onto a sheet of waxed paper to set. Let stand for 10 minutes, or until the chocolate has hardened completely and can be lifted off the waxed paper.

FUDGE FROSTING

YIELD: *1 to 1¼ cups*

2 ounces unsweetened chocolate, grated or finely chopped
½ cup butter or margarine
1¼ cups granulated sugar
½ cup milk
1 tablespoon light corn syrup
1 teaspoon chocolate or vanilla extract

1 In a saucepan over low heat, melt the chocolate and butter, stirring until smooth. Stir in the sugar, milk, and corn syrup. Bring to a boil. Boil for 2 to 3 minutes, or until smooth. Remove from the heat and cool for 5 minutes. Add the chocolate extract and using an electric mixer on low speed, beat until a spreadable consistency.

Grand marnier
SAUCE
YIELD: *1½ to 1¾ cups*
CHILL TIME: *30 minutes*

1 cup milk
2 large egg yolks
1 tablespoon granulated sugar
½ cup minus 1½ tablespoons
  chocolate ice cream
2 tablespoons Grand Marnier

1 In a small saucepan, over medium heat, warm the milk until bubbles start to form around the sides of the pan. Remove from the heat.

2 In a small bowl, using an electric mixer on medium speed, beat the egg yolks until thick and light-colored. Beat in the sugar. Pour the mixture into the top of a double boiler. Place over simmering water and beat in the hot milk, a little at a time. Continue beating 10 to 12 minutes, or until the mixture is thickened. Remove from the heat and stir in the ice cream and Grand Marnier. Pour into a small bowl. Cover and chill 30 minutes before using.

BAKING NOTES: Use chocolate ice cream for a chocolate Grand Marnier sauce.

Hot fudge sauce iv
YIELD : *1¼ cups*

1 cup half-and-half
8 ounces semi-sweet chocolate,
  grated or finely chopped
½ teaspoon chocolate or
  vanilla extract

1 In a saucepan over low heat, warm the cream until bubbles start to form around three sides of the pan. Add the chocolate, stirring until smooth. Cook over low heat, stirring slowly, until the mixture thickens slightly. Remove from the heat and stir in the chocolate extract. Serve hot over ice cream or other desserts.

Kahlúa cocoa
SAUCE
YIELD : *1⅓ cups*

½ cup water
½ cup Dutch processed cocoa powder
½ cup granulated sugar
¼ cup light corn syrup
2 tablespoons Kahlúa
1 teaspoon coffee liqueur

1 In a small saucepan, over medium heat, combine the water, cocoa powder, sugar and corn syrup. Bring to a boil, stirring constantly. Remove from heat. Stir in the Kahlúa and cool slightly. Stir in the liqueur. Serve warm or cold.

Low-fat
PASTRY SHELL
YIELD: *two 9-inch pie shells*
BAKING TIME: *10 minutes*

⅓ cup canola oil
1 tablespoon cider vinegar
2 cups all-purpose flour
½ teaspoon salt
2 to 3 tablespoons ice water

1 Position a rack in the center of the oven and preheat the oven to 425 degrees. Lightly grease a 9-inch pie pan.

2 Combine the canola oil and vinegar.

3 In a large bowl, combine the flour and salt. Using a fork, stir in the oil and vinegar until crumbly. Sprinkle the water over the top, a little at a time, and mix just until it makes a smooth dough.

4 On a lightly floured surface, roll one half of the dough out into a circle about ¼ inch thick. Transfer to the prepared pie pan and ease into the bottom and up the sides. Trim the edges and flute if desired. Line the crust with a piece of aluminum foil and fill with dried beans or pie weights.

5 Bake for 3 to 4 minutes, or until the crust feels set. Remove the foil and beans. Bake for 7 minutes, or until golden brown.

BAKING NOTES: Wrap remaining pastry shell dough in plastic wrap and place in the freezer for up to six months.

Raspberry sauce
Yield: *1³/₄ cups*

¼ cup raspberry liqueur
2 packages (10 ounces each) frozen
   raspberries, thawed

1 Combine the liqueur and raspberries in the container of a blender. Blend on high speed for 15 to 20 seconds. Strain the mixture through a sieve. Chill until ready to use.

Rum cream frosting
Yield: *2 to 2¹/₄ cups*

1 cup heavy cream
3 tablespoons powdered sugar
2 teaspoons dark rum

1 In a medium bowl, using an electric mixer on high speed, whip the cream until it starts to thicken. Gradually beat in the powdered sugar. Beat in the rum. Beat until soft peaks form. Spread over baked goods or use as a topping on fruit.

Strawberry glaze
Yield : *³/₄ cup*

1 cup fresh strawberries, hulled and
   mashed
2 tablespoons powdered sugar
2 teaspoons cornstarch or arrowroot

1 In a medium saucepan, over medium heat, combine the strawberries, powdered sugar, and cornstarch. Stirring constantly, cook until the mixture thickens. Remove from the heat. Cool completely before using.

Baking notes: Raspberries or blueberries can be used in place of the strawberries can be used in place of the strawberries. Fresh fruit is preferable but frozen fruit that is thawed and well drained can be substituted.

Chocolate leaves
Yield: *2 dozen leaves*
Chill time: *1 hour*

24 1½-inch long fresh-picked leaves
   (see Baking notes)
2 ounces semi-sweet chocolate,
   grated or finely chopped, or ½ cup
   semi-sweet chocolate chips
1 teaspoon butter or margarine
2 ounces almond bark

1 Thoroughly wash the leaves and pat dry with paper towels. Line a baking sheet with waxed or parchment paper.

2 In the top of a double boiler over simmering water, melt the chocolate and butter, stirring until smooth. Remove from the heat, leaving the top of the double boiler over the pan of hot water.

3 Using a pastry brush, spread the chocolate on the underside of the leaves, about ⅛ inch thick. Do not coat over the edges or it will be difficult to separate the chocolate from the leaves. Place the leaves on the prepared baking sheet and chill for 30 minutes to 1 hour, or until hard.

4 Starting at the stem end, carefully peel the leaves off the chocolate. Place the chocolate leaves on the baking sheet and chill until using.

HINTS FOR BAKING

1 Always read the recipe over at least once before starting.

2 Always use the very best ingredients you can afford.

3 Flour is the primary ingredient in baking and you should always have good quality flour on hand.

4 Unless stated otherwise, the oven should always be preheated before the item is placed in it.

5 Unless stated otherwise, it is assumed you will have the rack in the center position. If you are baking with more than one rack, remember the rack closest to the heat will have the greatest chance of browning or burning.

6 Completely cool a baking pan or baking sheet before reusing it.

7 Different oven controls react in different ways, therefore most baking temperatures given in recipes are suggestions only.

8 Unless stated otherwise, all ingredients should be at room temperature.

9 To measure 1/8 a teaspoon, first measure out 1/4 a teaspoon, then remove half of what you have measured out.

10 To measure honey, molasses or corn syrup, first lightly grease or oil the inside of the measuring device.

11 The measurement of nuts in recipes is usually considered whole. If a recipe calls for "1/2 cup of walnuts, ground," measure out 1/2 cup of the larger pieces and then grind them into smaller pieces. If it calls for ground walnuts, grind the nuts before measuring.

12 To prevent brown sugar from hardening, place a damp piece of cloth or paper towel in a small plastic bag, punch all over with a needle, and place in airtight container with the sugar.

13 When mixing in flour, do not add it all at once. It is best to add half of the flour and mix it in and then mix in the remainder, a little at a time.

14 If you are adding flour and liquids alternately, be sure the flour is the first and last ingredient added.

15 Store flour in an airtight container.

16 It is always best to sift flour before measuring, if a recipe calls for sifted flour.

17 Never use an aluminum bowl to beat egg whites. Copper is considered best, glass or ceramic are the next best to use.

18 When beating egg whites until stiff, the bowl and beaters must be clean and free of any grease or oil, or the egg whites can deflate.

19 It is best to use unsalted butter for baking. Remember that plain butter and margarine all contain salt. If you are going to use these products, the salt measurement in the recipe should be reduced. Butter-flavored shortening contains salt, but it is the best substitute for butter because of its blending and cooking qualities.

20 If butter is used in place of vegetable shortening, the amount of butter should be at least one quarter more than the amount of shortening.

21 Use regular stick margarine or butter, do not use the whipped, spread, or tub type, unless instructed to do so by the recipe.

22 For rich European-style pastries, use only butter.

23 When an alcoholic beverage is used to plump dried fruit, do not discard it after draining. It can be saved to use again or for flavoring in another recipe.

24 To chop sticky dried fruit, heat the knife or food chopper blades before using them.

25 When using dried herbs, the flavor may be brought out if you soak them in hot water for a few minutes.

26 Check liquid measures at eye level in a glass measuring cup.

27 When measuring with the standard measuring spoon, use a knife or spatula as a straight edge across the top.

28 Ovens should be preheated 12 to 20 minutes before using.

29 Shelled and unshelled nuts can attract insects. Store unshelled nuts in the refrigerator. Shelled nuts should be kept in the freezer.

30 Heat a lemon in a microwave for a few seconds before you squeeze it. It will produce more juice.

31 Always test for doneness after the minimum baking time. If a recipe tell you to bake something for 10 to 12 minutes, check it after 10 minutes.

32 To cream any mixture by hand, use the back of a large spoon until the mixture is soft and smooth.

33 When you stir, use a circular motion, not a beating motion or an over and under motion.

34 When a recipe says to beat in ingredients, use quick strokes in an over and under motion. Don't forget, when you are beating the mixture you will be adding air to it.

35 Do not melt chocolate in pieces smaller than 1-inch square over direct heat. Melt them in a pan or dish set over a pot of hot water.

36 It is best to cream butter by itself before adding the sugar.

37 Unless stated otherwise, use double acting baking powder.

38 For the very delicate butter-type cookies, use butter to grease the baking sheets.

39 To keep fruits and nuts from settling to the bottom of baked goods, dredge them in flour before adding them the batter.

40 A dark metal pan or baking sheet will bake faster than a shiny metal pan.

41 Glass containers cook baked goods faster than metal ones.

42 If baking more than one item in the oven at a time and using more than one shelf, stagger them rather than place them directly over each other. Be sure to allow for space between the item and the oven sides, back, and top for circulation of heat.

43 The best way to treat a first-degree burn from the oven or stove is to place ice cubes on it. Then check with a first aid guide or consult your doctor.

44 To rid pots and pans of flour wash them in warm water.

45 Egg whites should always be whipped at room temperature.

46 Always start to whip egg whites on a low speed and slowly increase the speed.

47 Dry wines are not compatible for use with fruit juices in baked goods, but sweet wines work very well.

48 Some ceramic bowls and dishes have a surface glaze that contains lead. After a short time, plastic tends to loose it surface shine and will absorb food and soap odors. For these reasons, it is best to use a metal or glass bowl.

49 It is not necessary to wash a flour sifter after each use. Simply place it in a plastic bag and tie it tightly closed.

50 When separating eggs, do it over a small bowl. Do not separate them over a bowl containing other recipe ingredients.

51 When making muffins, grease the muffin pans, rather than using paper baking cups. They will retard the muffins from rising.

52 Be careful not to stir muffin mixture when spooning the mixture into the pan, it will affect the finished product. Spoon the mixture only from the edge of the bowl.

53 When making doughnuts, if older dough is used to make the doughnuts, it will increase the frying time.

54 When making doughnuts, undermixed dough will usually produce a finished product that is rough in appearance. Overmixed dough will result in tough doughnuts.

55 If too much water is used in making a pie or pastry dough, the baked crust will be tough.

56 If milk is used in making pie or pastry dough, the crust will be less crisp.

57 Unless instructed otherwise, shortening should always be chilled when blended into the dough.

58 To reduce the unwanted juices in fruit pies, sprinkle cookie or cake crumbs over the bottom of the crust in the pie pan before adding the fruit.

59 For variations in fruit pies, spread a thin layer of pastry cream on the bottom, before the fruit is added.

60 To make an attractive fruit pie, save the best-looking slices of fruit for the top. Chop all of the fruit that is to go underneath the slices.

61 In open-face pies, when using hard fruit such as apples or pears, precook the fruit before adding to the pie. If you do not, the pie crust will cook before the fruit, and the bottom will be soggy.

62 After an open-faced fruit pie has been baked, brush the top fruit with a dessert glaze.

63 A greased baking sheet will cause puff pastry to spread. Line the pan with parchment paper in place of greasing.

64 If puff pastry is removed from the oven too soon, it may collapse.

65 Too much flour on a rolling surface can cause a pastry dough to become tough.

66 When rolling a pastry dough, use flour-dusted waxed paper. It won't be necessary to use as much flour.

67 Most pastry dough for pies should be rolled to a thickness of $\frac{1}{8}$ inch.

68 One way to avoid soggy bottom crusts in pies is to place the bottom of the pie pan closer to the heat; bake the pie on the lowest rack in the oven.

69 Do not add hot fillings to unbaked pie crusts.

70 When making a pie filling, always add the sugar or lemon juice after the filling has been heated and thickened.

71 Pumpkin pie filling should be allowed to stand untouched for 30 minutes before being poured into the pie shell.

72 When preparing cream-style pies, do not use too much unflavored gelatin or the filling will be rubbery.

73 Do not use raw, uncooked pineapple or papaya with gelatin. Precook it first.

74 On the average, it should take from 8 to 10 minutes to properly cream butter and sugar using the slow or medium speed of a hand-held electric mixer. Do not use high speed to cream the two ingredients.

75 When melted chocolate is added to a batter, add it immediately after creaming the fat and sugar and before any eggs or liquid.

76 On average, it takes no less than 5 minutes to beat eggs into a cake batter.

77 When adding dry ingredients to cake batters, do it one third at a time, alternating with half of the liquids, beginning and ending with the dry ingredients.

78 Usually beaten egg whites are the last ingredient added to a cake batter.

79 Slightly warmed eggs can be beaten to a greater volume than cold ones.

80 Too hot an oven will cause a cake to set unevenly with a humped center. Too cool an oven causes poor volume and texture.

81 Unless instructed otherwise, always cool cake layers completely before assembling and icing.

82 Excessive crowns (humps) on cakes should be sliced off with a serrated knife before icing.

83 When assembling a cake, where the filling is different from the frosting, do not spread the filling over the edge of the cake.

84 In warmer climates, substitute fondant icings for buttercream icings.

85 When making cookies, remember that most crisp cookies are made from very stiff doughs.

86 A high sugar content in a cookie dough increases the chance of excessive spreading while baking.

87 Using fine grain sugar in cookie doughs will decrease the chance of spreading.

88 A large amount of baking soda in a cookie dough causes spreading, as does over creaming of the sugar and fat.

89 There is a greater chance of a cookie dough spreading if the oven temperature is too low.

90 In most cookie baking, the degree of doneness is indicated by the color of the baked cookie.

91 When making pudding, if the milk is scalded before being added it will reduce the cooking time.

92 Leftover cakes and other baked desserts can be dried as you would dry bread crumbs and used as a garnish on other dessert items and baked goods. Chocolate cake is particularly good for this. Leave the cake out in the air for 24 to 36 hours, or until it becomes very hard. Then crush or pulse into a fine crumb using hand grinder or food processor.

93 Don't rely only on baking times for checking the doneness of cakes. To test if a cake is finished baking, always check the look, smell, sound, and feel. It will pull slightly away from the sides of the pan, it will have a distinct aroma, the sounds of air bubbles popping in the cake will have slowed, and it will spring back when gently touched.

94 Always start to check for doneness with a cake about 10 minutes before the recommended baking time has passed.

95 Unless stated otherwise, most cakes should be cooled for 5 to 10 minutes in the pan set on a wire rack before inverting onto a wire rack or plate to finish cooling.

96 When a cake is to be frozen or stored in the refrigerator, always wrap it securely in waxed paper and then in a plastic wrap or aluminum foil. Large selfsealing plastic bags are ideal for this purpose.

97 Be sure the icing, frosting, or garnish that is placed on a cake complements the flavor of the cake.

98 Cheesecakes will often crack on the top if they are cooked in too hot an oven.

99 Even in the best recipes in the world, chocolate is a very difficult ingredient to work with. Be sure you understand it before you try to work with it. (See Chocolate and Cocoa Section.)

100 When adding a lot of liquids to melted chocolate, stir fast and add the liquid all at once.

101 If chocolate stiffens or thickens, heating alone will not thin chocolate.

102 When cutting marshmallows, use scissors by dipping them in hot water, and they will not stick to the blade.

CHOCOLATE AND COCOA

Both chocolate and cocoa are edible ingredients produced from the cacao bean. After the beans are picked they are fermented, roasted, and ground. The end product is known as chocolate liquor. Included in the liquor is the yellow fat called cocoa butter. Once obtained, there are six types of food products or ingredients that can be processed from the chocolate liquor: cocoa or what we know as unsweetened cocoa powder, bitter chocolate, sweet chocolate, milk chocolate, cocoa butter, and finally white chocolate.

Cocoa is a dry powder. It is what is left after most of the cocoa butter has been removed from chocolate liquor. *Dutch processed cocoa powder* is a product that has been processed with alkali and is usually slightly darker in color. The flavor is more delicate and it is more easily dissolved in liquids, such as hot water or milk. Dutch processed cocoa is usually neutral or slightly alkaline and will not react with baking soda in a recipe. Therefore baking powder must be used as the leavening agent in a recipe.

When baking with cocoa, if not enough baking powder is used in the recipe the finished product can range in color from light tan to a dark brown depending on the amount of cocoa powder added. If too much baking powder is used, the color will be a reddish-brown and this is usually only desirable in a devil's food cake.

It is important to remember that there are differences between various brands of cocoa powder, including Dutch processed cocoa powders. Should it be necessary to switch from one brand of cocoa powder to another, it is recommended to experiment first to see if you will have the same results.

Non-Dutch processed cocoa powder is usually called natural cocoa and is more acidic. When it is used to make cakes and other baked goods it is possible to use baking soda as part of the leavening. All cocoa powders will keep for an extended period of time if stored in airtight containers with moistureproof covers.

One thing to remember is that cocoa powder also contains starch, and starch will tend to absorb the moisture in a batter. So, if you want to add cocoa powder to a yellow cake recipe to make it a chocolate cake, the amount of flour should be reduced to compensate for the added starch.

Bitter chocolate or *unsweetened chocolate* as it is also known, is the same as chocolate liquor. It contains no sugar and is bitter to the taste. For a chocolate liquor to be classified as unsweetened it must contain 50 to 58 percent cocoa butter. There are several qualities of unsweetened chocolate on the market. The least expensive brands have usually removed most of the cocoa butter and replaced it with a coconut oil or inexpensive vegetable shortening.

Sweet chocolate is unsweetened chocolate that has sugar

added and the cocoa butter has been adjusted in varying proportions. If the amount of sugar is low, then it may be referred to as semisweet. If the sugar is less than for semisweet, it will be called bittersweet. In both cases it must contain at least 35 percent chocolate liquor and the sugar content will range from 35 to 50 percent. At the same time a product labeled sweet chocolate may contain as little as 15 percent chocolate liquor.

When using sweet chocolate as a candy coating, the chocolate must be prepared by a process called tempering. This is nothing more than melting the chocolate without letting it get too hot, then reducing the temperature to a predetermined acceptable level, and rewarming it a second time. There are less expensive chocolates available for this procedure. They have had part of the cocoa butter replaced with vegetable shortening or coconut oil. They are easier to handle and they don't require tempering. The products are usually sold under the names of Chocolate Coating, Cake Coating, Candy Coating, and even Baking Chocolate. Read the label carefully to determine if the product is right for you.

Milk chocolate is like sweet chocolate only milk solids have been added. Although it may be purchased in edible bar forms, it is also used to coat various other types of candies. Because of its low taste factor it is seldom melted and incorporated into baked goods.

Cocoa butter is the fat that is pressed out of the chocolate liquor during processing. It is seldom available in supermarkets and its primary use is in bake shops and candy making facilities where it is used for thinning coating chocolate.

White chocolate isn't really a chocolate in that it contains no chocolate liquor. Usually it is made from cocoa butter (and that is where the name chocolate is derived from), sugar, and milk solids. It is used for making candies, decorations, and occasionally to make frostings for baked goods. A less expensive type and variety of this product is readily available. It is often called almond bark.

Chocolate should be stored in a cool, dry place with a constant temperature between 60 to 75 degrees. The key word is dry; the humidity should not be more than 50 percent. When refrigerated, chocolate must be wrapped tightly in an airtight bag or container. If it is left unwrapped it can absorb moisture that will condense when the chocolate is removed from the refrigerator. It can also absorb unwanted odors from other items in the refrigerator. Most chocolate, if kept tightly wrapped, can keep in the refrigerator for 6 months or more, but it is advised that the chocolate be used as soon after purchasing as possible. Some experts say that chocolate cannot be kept in the freezer. Those who say it can be frozen, say it can keep up to 4 months with no change in the flavor or texture.

On occasion a candy bar or baking chocolate will have a grayish white film, like a mold on the surface. This is called "bloom." Bloom usually develops when chocolate has been exposed to fluctuations in temperature. While bloom may look unattractive, it is safe to eat. If the chocolate is melted, it will loose the bloom.

It is easy to become confused when substituting cocoa for chocolate. The primary difference between cocoa and unsweetened chocolate is that cocoa has much less cocoa butter. Usually extra vegetable shortening or oil will be necessary when substituting cocoa powder for chocolate. There is one problem in using regular shortening as a replacement for cocoa butter. Shortening has about twice the shortening power of cocoa butter. Because of all the various cocoa powders available, there is no single substitution ratio for all of them. Most brands of cocoa powder do include substitution directions on their packaging, so check the label.

MELTING CHOCOLATE

The melting of chocolate is critical to the success of a recipe and there are many ways that chocolate can be melted. Always grate, chop, or shave chocoate before melting it. When heating chocolate, use a metal spoon and stir frequently in a circular motion until the chocolate is melted and smooth. Do not use an over and under motion with the spoon because this might add air to the chocolate. Any of the following methods can be used, but the first two are highly recommended.

1 Hot-Water Bath Method: Place the chocolate in a clean dry metal bowl or top of a double boiler. Place over a larger bowl or pan that contains hot water. The water should not be boiling. When the chocolate starts to melt,

use a metal spoon and stir in a circular motion. (It may be necessary to hold one edge of the bowl while stirring.) After the chocolate is completely melted and smooth, remove from the water and set aside until ready to use. If the chocolate is to be used for dipping, leave it over the warm water. It may be necessary to refresh the warm water before you are ready to use the chocolate. While this method is usually the slowest, there is less chance of scorching the chocolate.

2 Double Boiler Method: Place the chocolate in the top of the double boiler, being sure the pan is dry and free of any moisture. Place water in the bottom pan. Place the top pan with the chocolate in it into the bottom pan and place over low heat. Stir constantly until the chocolate is melted. Do not allow the water in the bottom pan to touch the top pan as this could overheat the chocolate. Do not place a cover on the top pan as moisture might collect inside of the cover and drop into the chocolate. If this happens the chocolate might sieze and thicken. If a single drop of moisture falls into the chocolate, carefully lift the drop out with a metal spoon. When the chocolate is melted, remove the top pan from the bottom one and set aside until ready to use. If the chocolate is to be used for dipping, leave the top pan over the bottom pan off the burner. The water in the bottom pan must be kept lukewarm. When the water cools, replace it with warm water.

3 Direct Heat Method: Place the chocolate in a small saucepan and working quickly over low heat, stir constantly until the chocolate is melted and smooth. This method is

very fast but has a greater chance of failure. Chocolate burns at such a low temperature that unless you are very experienced with melting chocolate, this method is not recommended.

4 Microwave Method: Place the chopped chocolate in a small microwave safe bowl and microwave, uncovered, on medium power for 1 to 2 minutes. Remove from the microwave and stir with a metal spoon. The chocolate will not become liquid while in the oven. As a matter of fact it will retain its shape until stirred. It will be shiny when it is ready to be stirred. If after the first heating the chocolate hasn't melted sufficiently or is a little lumpy, return it to the oven for another 20 to 30 seconds. It is recommended that medium power be used until you have become accustomed to melting chocolate in a microwave.

TEMPERING CHOCOLATE

The more one gets into the wonderful world of chocolate, the more they will hear the term tempering. The most important use for tempered chocolate is in candy making, for dipping or coating other items. It is really a very simple procedure, but at the same time one of the most important. It only involves three steps: melting, tempering, and rewarming.

In the melting step the chocolate is melted using one of the above methods. Stir the chocolate gently and use a thermometer to check the temperature frequently. Immerse the bulb of the thermometer completely in the chocolate, being careful that it does not touch the pan. Let sit for 1 minute before taking a reading. During this process, the temperature of the chocolate is raised to 115 to 118 degrees. (NOTE: it is important to remember that not all chocolate is alike and the manufacturers of various chocolates will recommend different temperatures for their chocolate. One European manufacturer recommends that its chocolate be melted at 122 degrees.)

In the tempering step, cooling or precrystalling occurs. After the chocolate is melted, it is removed from the heat, set in a cool place, and stirred constantly but slowly so no air is incorporated until it reaches 78 to 79 degrees on a thermometer. Although most manufacturers of chocolate recommend a slow cooling, pastry chefs will usually speed up the process by setting the pan or bowl containing the hot chocolate over a larger container of cold water.

By the time the chocolate has cooled to the proper temperature, it is too thick for dipping or other uses and must be warmed and melted a second time. The chocolate is rewarmed using one of the above melting methods until the temperature of the chocolate is 86 to 88 degrees. Rewarming is the most important step. At no time should the chocolate be allowed to rise above the recommended temperature. If it does, the process will have to be repeated all over again.

Some additional tips for melting and tempering chocolate are:

1 First and foremost, do not allow any water, even a drop, to come into contact with the chocolate.

2 If the pan or bowl you are using to melt or temper chocolate is too thin, it might transfer heat too fast and subsequently burn the chocolate.

3 Do not rush to melt the chocolate by increasing the temperature. If you do, it might curdle and thicken. If this does happen, add a little vegetable shortening. Do not add butter or margarine.

4 Do not substitute semisweet or milk chocolate for unsweetened chocolate in a recipe.

5 When working with melted or tempered chocolate use a wooden spoon or metal spatula.

6 When working with tempered chocolate, the work area should be cool; 65 to 68 degrees is the ideal temperature.

7 In hot or warm weather, if the chocolate seems too thick, the addition of melted wax will help the chocolate resist the heat. One-half ounce of melted wax should be sufficient for $\frac{1}{2}$ pound of chocolate.

PREMELTED CHOCOLATE

Premelted unsweetened chocolate was introduced into the baking market a few years ago. It is used as a convenient alternative to blocks of chocolate that are subsequently chopped or grated and then melted. Premelted unsweetened chocolate is a mixture of unsweetened cocoa powder and vegetable oil that is sealed in premeasured servings in a foil pouch. It is used primarily for flavoring in cakes, cookies, and other baked goods.